Kid
in the
Kitchen

Melissa Clark

with Daniel Gercke

photographs by David Malosh

**100 recipes
and tips
for young
home cooks**

Kid
in the
Kitchen

clarkson potter/publishers NEW YORK

For every kid who
dares to dream big
in the kitchen. You
know who you are.

Library of Congress Cataloging-in-Publication Data
is available upon request.

ISBN 978-0-593-23228-6
Ebook ISBN 978-0-593-23229-3

Printed in the United States

Photographer: David Malosh
Food Stylist: Simon Andrews
Prop Stylist: Paige Hicks

Editors: Doris Cooper and Lydia O'Brien
Designers: Stephanie Huntwork and Jan Derevjanik
Cover designer: Stephanie Huntwork
Creative Director: Marysarah Quinn
Illustrator: Meighan Cavanaugh
Icon illustrators: nemlaza, Leremy, and JaynaKubat
via Shutterstock
Production Editor: Terry Deal
Production Manager: Kim Tyner
Production Director: Derek Gullino
Composition: Merri Ann Morrell
Copy Editor: Katherine Ness
Proofreaders: Natalie Blachere,
Kathy Brock, Jonathan Milder, and
Maria Zizka
Indexer: Elizabeth Parson

10 9 8 7 6 5 4 3 2 1

First Edition

Contents

Hi!

If you love to eat, you should learn how to cook. Because no one cooks or eats exactly like you do. You have your own tastes and needs. Maybe you need school snacks and after-school snacks. Maybe you want to cook for sleepovers or video game parties. The things you're into aren't always what grown-ups are into. Your tastes may change and evolve, but you definitely have strong opinions about what's good. And learning how to make food YOU think is good is what this book is about.

If you love to eat, you should learn how to cook.

Making the food I wanted, when I wanted it, was why I baked my first cake without any help at the age of eight. I desperately craved a purple layer cake with rainbow sprinkles, and there was no way my mom was going to make it for me when it wasn't my birthday. So I dug out the *Joy of Cooking* and made a floury mess, dyeing the batter with red and blue food coloring. It turned the batter a lovely shade of lavender–and I ate so much of it that my tongue and fingers turned lavender, too (yum). But when I took the cake out of the oven, it baked up into a scary shade of gray. And, apparently, I forgot to add the baking powder, because it was flat as a flip-flop. But I frosted it in violet-tinted buttercream and topped it with sprinkles. I was psyched to share it with my best friend, Kimmy, who lived down the block. We thought the gray flip-flop cake tasted amazing.

So, yeah, I've come a long way since then. I write cookbooks and recipes for *The New York Times* for a living, and now most of what I cook turns out pretty well. When it's flat and gray, it's flat and gray on purpose.

But ever since sharing that flip-flop cake with Kimmy, I realized that one surefire way to make myself–and my friends and family–really happy was to make (and share) the food I loved to eat. Cooking never fails to bring joy. I strongly believe that everyone who loves to eat should learn to cook.

That flip-flop cake taught me another lesson, too: Cooking isn't about getting things perfect–it's about having fun (and licking the bowl) while you do it.

You do have to learn some basics to get going. Every dish has a few fundamental steps that will make it work. In this book, I take you step-by-step through the process of understanding and making a recipe. You'll find a set of rock-solid starting points that will help you cook exactly what you want to eat. The Tips & Tweaks will teach you how to adapt each recipe to suit your current mood or that of the people you are cooking for.

So I hope you'll mess around with these recipes, hack them, hype them, make them yours. As long as you've got the basics and you're having fun, whatever you make is bound to be delicious!

Now get in that kitchen and own it!

—Your friend, Melissa

How to Cook

1 Read the recipe all the way through and answer this four-part question:

- **Does this dish sound delicious?**
  (No? Pick another recipe that does.)

- **use ingredients and equipment that I have?**
  (No? Go shopping or pick another recipe.)

- **have steps that I know how to do?**
  (No? Ask an adult or do some internet research.)

- **fit my schedule?**
  (If the total prep and cooking time is too long, save it for tomorrow.)

If you answered yes, yes, yes, and yes, then you're good! Do your research and shopping, **then read the whole recipe one more time** to rehearse all the steps in your head.

2 **Plan for the right amount.** If the dish serves four, you can halve all the ingredients to serve two, or double them to serve eight. Math skills! You also might need to adjust the cooking times slightly, so when you make changes it's even more important to watch the doneness cues of the recipe rather than just the timing.

3 **Wash your hands well with soap**—the unwritten first step of every recipe in the universe.

4 **Heat the oven** if the recipe calls for it (make sure there's nothing in it first, though!).

5 **Set out every single ingredient in the recipe.** Trust me, this is the only way to make sure you don't leave an ingredient behind as you get into cooking beast mode.

6 **Chop and measure** all of your ingredients before cooking, and put them into little bowls, so you can just dump them in as needed. This makes cooking shockingly speedy.

7 **Clean as you go.** Set out a couple of kitchen towels and a sponge or rag to wipe your hands and surfaces between steps. If you clean what you can while the water boils or the dough chills, you'll have less to do at the end. Future you will thank you.

8 **Taste as you cook.** It's important to test whether the food needs more of something, like salt or lemon juice, while it's still cooking. This is also a great way to get a sense of how ingredients change as they cook.

9 **Manage the heat.** Make pans on the stovetop less bumpable by turning pot handles AWAY from you while they cook. Put oven mitts where you can easily grab them when you need to. Stay alert to everything that's happening in the kitchen and put your phone away. Phone-checking is the enemy of cooking, and the friend of burnt garlic.

10 **Clean up well when you're done.** Wash pots and pans, wipe down work surfaces, put everything back in its place, and sweep the floor. Leaving everything as shiny and clean as before you started is like a magic trick. Mess? What mess?

Any Recipe

Chop Like A Pro

Knives are sharp and can be dangerous, but when you hold them correctly and pay close attention, the work goes safely and quickly.

1. Use a wooden or plastic cutting board that is stable and big enough to hold what you're chopping. You can keep the cutting board from slipping by putting a wet paper towel under it. It should not move or slip while you're cutting.

2. Hold the handle of the knife close to the blade. Now put your thumb on the side of the metal blade, and your forefinger on the other side. By pinching your thumb and forefinger, you have a lot of control over the blade.

3. Hold your ingredients with your hand in claw position, fingertips curled under and away from the blade of the knife. This keeps your fingertips safe (there are so many gory stories of chefs cutting off the tips of their fingers when they're careless). Lead with the joint of your middle finger. I suggest asking an experienced adult or watching a couple of online videos about how to hold a knife and how to chop. It's easy to understand once you see it up close in action.

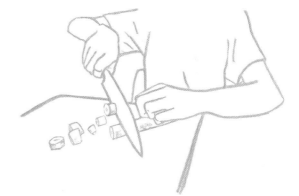

Onion Prep

Start by placing the onion on a cutting board and cutting it in half from the root end to the pointy tip, steadying it with your other hand. (A) Now you can peel off the papery skin. Place the flat side down on the cutting board and dice, chop, or slice as your recipe calls for.

HIP TIP: It really helps to watch a video, and there are lots online.

DICED

Hold the knife parallel to the cutting board and make horizontal cuts about ¼ inch apart, stopping at least ½ inch before the root. Make sure to hold your steadying hand away from the path of the blade. The root end will hold everything together as you go. (B)

Next, make vertical cuts about ¼ inch apart, cutting from the tip end almost to the root, but stop at least ½ inch away from the root. Everything is still held together by the root. (C)

Finally, slice the onion crosswise, at ¼-inch intervals. Stop ½ inch or more from the root end. (D)

CHOPPED

Dice the onion as described above, then chop the pieces by rocking the knife over them until they are slightly finer.

SLICED

Cut off the tip of the onion, but leave the root end intact. Hold the knife and the onion as described in Chop Like a Pro (page 11), and slice to the desired thickness.

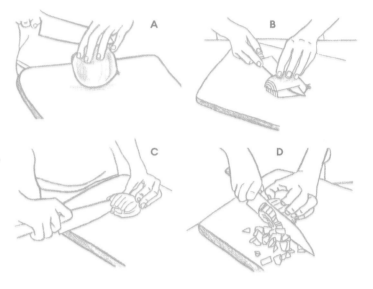

NOTE: Freshly cut onions get back at you by making you cry. Their juices produce a gas (syn-propanethial-S-oxide, if you were wondering) that can make many people's eyes sting and tear up. Don't worry though, there are a few things you can do:

● **Cut near a fan.** The fan disperses the gas before it reaches your eyes.

● **Don't cut too close to the root end.** The concentration of sulphur at the root amps up that irritating gas.

● **Wear goggles.** I now own special onion goggles, but I have been spotted wearing swim and even ski goggles in the company of a chopped onion.

● **Don't touch your face.** Learn to scratch that itchy cheek with your shoulder!

Garlic Prep

PEEL & CUT

For mincing, slicing, or grating: Pull off an individual clove from the head, and place it on a cutting board. Rest the flat side of a chef's knife on top of it, and gently push down until you hear the papery covering of the garlic split. Don't smash it flat, just enough to loosen the peel. Pull off the papery covering–if it still won't come off, re-squish the clove. Cut off the dry root end.

ONCE IT'S PEELED, YOU CAN:

- **thinly slice** the clove crosswise (if you need it to be more stable, halve it vertically first)

- **mince** it by slicing it and then rocking a chef's knife back and forth across the pieces until you get a consistency like coarse sand

- **grate** it on a Microplane or other fine grater

SMASH & PEEL

To add a mild and sweet garlic flavor: Place the clove on a cutting board. Rest the flat side of a chef's knife on top of it and give it a good thwack with the heel of your hand. The clove should be crushed pretty flat and the peel should pull off easily. Cut off the root end of the clove and it's ready to throw in a pan with roasting veggies. Discard the clove after cooking.

weigh it up

Some baking recipes, like the ones in this book, give measurements in cups as well as grams. If you have a scale, always weigh. You put the bowl on the scale and press "tare," or zero, button to get started (to subtract the weight of the bowl). Then after you add each ingredient, you hit the tare button again so you start back at zero (this avoids the math of adding up the grams as you go). Easy!

There's also a lot less cleanup when you use a scale–I don't have to dirty as many (or any!) measuring cups and spoons, and it makes the whole thing go so much faster. It's what the professional bakers do, and they don't mess around.

It's okay if you don't have a scale, though. My baked goods come out fine using measuring cups and spoons. Here's a tip for using a measuring cup for flour: stir the flour with a spoon to make sure it hasn't compacted before you scoop it with the measuring cup. Compacted flour would give you too much. For all my recipes, 1 cup of flour equals 125 grams, while compacted flour can weigh as much as 140 grams per cup.

measure well

Measure your ingredients into prep bowls before you start cooking. Use measuring spoons and cups–you need a set of measuring cups for dry ingredients and a separate, liquid measuring cup, because they are slightly different.

SAUTÉ PAN or SKILLET

Go with one 10-inch.

SAUCEPANS

Get a small 1-quart and a medium 3-quart.

RIMMED BAKING SHEETS

One or two.

The 20 (or So) Tools
to Cook Almost Anything

CHEF'S KNIFE

The common 8-inch version should work, but you may be more comfortable with a 6-inch knife. Don't use a knife that feels too big or heavy to control. It should feel like an extension of your hand.

PARING KNIFE

CUTTING BOARD

Wood or plastic.

PEELER

MIXING BOWLS

Stainless-steel nesting bowls are lightweight and easy to clean. You'll want two or three different sizes.

WHISK

COLANDER

MEASURING CUPS & SPOONS

At least one full set of each.

OVEN MITTS THAT FIT YOUR HANDS

The mitten-type is best, giving you the most coverage. Never use a kitchen towel as a pot holder—it can slip.

FLEXIBLE SPATULA

Either rubber or heatproof silicone.

WOODEN SPOON

TIMER

One that you can control with wet or gloppy hands (so, not your phone).

These tools are all you need to cook most recipes. But always read a new recipe carefully to see what equipment you need *before* starting. There's nothing worse than breezing through Steps one and two, only to realize you don't have a whisk for Step three.

Also useful:

DUTCH OVEN

A big cast-iron pot with a lid.

COOKIE SHEET

Cookies! In a pinch you can use rimmed baking sheets.

COOLING RACK

To help hot things cool off quickly so they don't overcook.

RULER

To measure your chopping and dicing and to measure pans.

MICROPLANE or OTHER FINE GRATER

Easier to control than a box grater and better for things like garlic, fresh ginger, and citrus zest.

PREP BOWLS

Little bowls to hold ingredients that you've chopped or measured. Any bowl will do, but it's good to have several at the ready.

SALAD SPINNER

An amusement park ride for lettuce. There are other ways to dry washed greens but none as effective or fun as the spinner.

LADLE

INSTANT-READ THERMOMETER

Digital or old-school.

KITCHEN SHEARS

Special scissors used only for cooking. Don't get paper dust on your pizza.

Insta Your Dish
Food Photography Hacks & Tips

Now that you've cooked it, maybe you want to show it off. Here are some tips for taking stunning food photos that will show off your cooking to its best advantage. Say cheese, Grilled Cheese!

Food Styling Counts

Arrange the plate so your dish's most awesome qualities are front and center.

Load the plate carefully. Don't let the food look glopped on. Slice the food if it looks better.

Plan ahead for color. A lot of perfectly tasty food is the same shade of brown or beige, so have some different colors on the plate. A bright vegetable or a little chopped parsley can go a long way.

Hold back on the sauce. To let the shape and texture of the food come through, use less sauce for the picture than you would otherwise.

Get That Shot

Now that your food is styled, it's time to shoot. Here are a few tips from Melanie Dunea, star professional food photographer, to make your hard work shine.

Use natural light, either from a window or by shooting outside, to bring out better color and subtle shading.

Use different surfaces as a background. Your tabletop, a large cutting board, a cloth napkin, a baking tray, even the floor can help food look its best.

Try the photo from multiple angles. Directly overhead can be great, but also experiment with various angles and heights to find the one that makes your dish look the most delicious.

Add a prop. A cloth napkin can add color, a glass and silverware can give a sense of the table and set the scene.

Keep the shot simple. The focus needs to be on the food, not the props or background.

Clean your lens with a napkin or cloth, especially phone lenses. A clean lens makes for a sharper picture.

Make sure you can't see your shadow in the frame.

The photo doesn't have to look perfect. It's about showing how you feel about what you're about to eat.

Have fun! It will show in your photo.

Here are the key terms that will help you decode every recipe in this book.

Kitchen

Cutting

Peel ● Take off the outer skin or rind from a fruit or vegetable. For thin skins, like apples or carrots, use a vegetable peeler. For citrus, use a paring knife and your fingers. And, of course, you know how to peel a banana.

Zest ● Use a Microplane, a zester, or the small holes of a box grater to take off only the colored outer layer of citrus. That's where all the flavor is–the white pith underneath can be bitter!

Chop ● Cut the ingredient into chunks with a knife. How big? Usually ¼- to ½-inch pieces. "Coarsely chopped" means ½- to ¾-inch pieces, like a chickpea or a little larger. "Finely chopped" means ⅛- to ¼-inch pieces, like lentils or a little smaller.

Slice ● Cut the ingredient into even slices. The thickness is usually indicated in the recipe, but if it's not, ⅛ inch is standard.

Dice ● Cut the ingredient into ¼-inch cubes. There are special methods for dicing some ingredients, like onions. See Chop Like a Pro, page 11.

Mince ● Like chopping, but even smaller: cut ⅛-inch pieces or smaller. Think grains of rice small.

Grate ● Cut the ingredient, like cheese or garlic, with a Microplane or other handheld grater, or the small holes of a box grater, or a food processor.

Shred ● Cut the ingredient with the large holes on a box grater, or a food processor. It's like grating except the pieces are usually bigger.

Stir ● Combine the ingredients with a wooden spoon or a flexible spatula, using a steady circular motion.

Fold ● Gently combine ingredients (usually beaten egg whites or whipped cream). Plunge a spatula or spoon to the bottom of the bowl and carefully bring the contents of the bottom to the top, repeating until the ingredient you are folding in is just incorporated but not overmixed.

Whisk ● Fully, and energetically, combine the ingredients with a whisk.

Decoder

Combining

Beat ● Combine really energetically with a whisk or an electric mixer to mix the ingredients and add a little air into the mixture.

Whip ● Combine really, really energetically with a whisk or electric mixer. The higher speed works to add enough air to fluff up things like whipped cream or egg whites.

Knead ● In bread baking, kneading helps the dough come together and activates the gluten in the dough, which helps the bread rise. (See How to Knead Dough, page 223.)

Toss ● Gently combine the ingredients with a liquid (like lettuce and salad dressing or potatoes about to be roasted and olive oil), using two forks, tongs, or your clean hands to coat the ingredients all over.

Scrape ● Use a rubber spatula to move all the ingredients to one side or out of a bowl.

Simmer ● Heat a liquid until small bubbles float to the surface and barely seem to pop.

Boil ● Heat a liquid until it is vigorously bubbling and the surface is "rolling."

Heating

Bake or roast ● Baking and roasting are the same thing: place your ingredient or ingredients in the oven and let the hot, dry air cook them.

Broil ● Sear the ingredient one side at a time with intense heat, either in an oven broiler or on a grill.

Heat "until shimmering" ● Heat oil in a pan until it moves easily across the bottom. Watch carefully and you'll see the change as the oil gets runnier.

Sauté ● Heat a thin or minced ingredient quickly in a hot pan, often with a bit of oil or butter. *Sauté* is French for "jumped," and that's sometimes what the ingredients seem to be doing while they cook.

Panfry ● Like sautéing, but with a larger ingredient, like meat, with lower heat and more oil or butter. Panfrying gives great browning and crispness to foods but without the large amount of oil used for deep-frying.

Stir-fry ● Heat bite-size ingredients in a hot pan with oil, stirring constantly.

Deep-fat fry ● Cook the ingredient by submerging it in hot oil.

Reheat ● Heat a dish that has already been cooked and cooled. Best done slowly in a 300°F oven or in a microwave.

Breakfast & Brunch

Waffles Worth the Wait

Yeasted waffles have the best texture and tang. The fermentation of the yeast builds flavor by adding just a little bit of acidity and adds lightness by creating tiny pockets of air. This batter rises overnight, so when you wake up, all you have to do is cook the waffles and you'll be ready to go. Or else mix it up in the morning and let it rise for 2 to 3 hours at room temperature.

(See Weigh It Up, page 13.)

2¼ cups / 540 grams **milk**

½ cup / 1 stick / 113 grams **unsalted butter,** cut into cubes, plus more for the waffle iron and for serving

1 tablespoon / 12 grams **sugar,** plus a pinch for the yeast

1 teaspoon / 6 grams **kosher salt**

½ cup / 118 grams **lukewarm water** (it should feel only slightly warm when you stick a finger in—not at all hot)

1 packet / 2½ teaspoons / 7 grams **active dry yeast,** or 1¾ teaspoons / 5 grams instant yeast

2¾ cups / 345 grams **all-purpose flour**

2 large **eggs**

¼ teaspoon **baking soda**

Maple syrup or jam, for serving (for more toppings, see Tips & Tweaks)

get it set

SPECIAL EQUIPMENT: Waffle iron, pastry brush

Set out all your ingredients except for the eggs and baking soda.

1. In a small pot, combine the milk and butter. Place the pot over medium-high heat and let it cook until the butter melts and the mixture is hot but not simmering, 2 to 3 minutes. Stir in the tablespoon of sugar and the salt; set aside until lukewarm.

2. In a large bowl, combine the lukewarm water, the yeast, and the pinch of sugar. Let it sit for a few minutes, until it starts to get a little frothy; that's the yeast getting active (for more about yeast, see Rise Up! The Science of Bread, page 217).

3. Whisk the milk mixture into the yeast mixture until well combined, then whisk in the flour. Cover the bowl with a plate, pot lid, or plastic wrap, and let it stand until the batter has doubled in volume: overnight in the refrigerator, or 2 to 3 hours at room temperature.

4. If you're not going to serve the waffles the minute they come off the waffle iron, heat your oven to 200°F and put an ovenproof platter or a sheet pan in it.

5. Heat up your waffle iron. Whisk the eggs and baking soda into the risen waffle batter. It will deflate a little, and that is okay.

6. Using a pastry brush, lightly coat the waffle iron with butter. Cook the waffles (using about ½ cup batter per waffle–but check the instructions for your particular model) until golden and crisp. Most waffle irons have a light that tells you when the waffles are done, but the best indicator that the waffles are ready is when the steam stops rising from the appliance. Use tongs to transfer the waffles either to waiting plates or to the platter or sheet pan in the oven to keep warm. Butter the iron between batches as needed. Serve the waffles with more butter if you like, and with maple syrup or jam.

tips & tweaks

● Don't add things like blueberries or chocolate chips to waffle batter; they can stick to the waffle iron and burn.

● Be super-creative with the toppings. All kinds of things are good *on* a waffle, like:

- Lemon curd
- Confectioners' sugar
- Honey
- Whipped cream
- Chopped nuts
- Sliced fruit
- Nutella
- Hot Fudge Sauce (page 179)
- Butterscotch Sauce (page 180)

Levitating Dutch Baby

"Dutch baby" is a mysterious name for a big puffy pancake that tastes amazingly light. Steam from the wet ingredients gets trapped in pockets of elastic eggy batter, inflating them like a bubble. The pancake will gently fall before it reaches the table, but it will keep its airy, light texture. Make it sweet for breakfast or dessert, or savory for brunch or dinner. Whichever you decide to cook, it will fly off the plate.

4 large **eggs**, at room temperature

¾ cup / 180 grams **whole milk** (nondairy is fine), at room temperature

¾ teaspoon finely grated **lemon zest** (optional)

Pinch of **fine sea salt**

¾ cup / 94 grams **all-purpose flour**

4 tablespoons / ½ stick / 57 grams **unsalted butter**

make it sweet

⅓ cup / 66 grams **granulated sugar**

½ cup / 113 grams **confectioners' sugar**

2 tablespoons / 30 grams **fresh lemon juice**

or make it savory

⅓ cup / 35 grams **grated Parmesan cheese**, plus more for serving

1 tablespoon chopped **fresh thyme leaves** or other herbs

¼ teaspoon **freshly ground black pepper**

get it set

Take the eggs and milk out of the fridge 30 to 60 minutes ahead to let them come to room temperature. (See When Not to Be Chill, page 255.)

Set out all your ingredients.

Heat the oven to 425°F.

1. In a large bowl, whisk together the eggs, milk, lemon zest if using, and sea salt. Vigorously whisk in the flour until the batter is smooth and nearly lump-free. This might take a minute to get most of the lumps out (a few small ones are fine). If you're going for a sweet pancake, whisk in the granulated sugar. For a savory one, whisk in the Parmesan, thyme, and black pepper. (Alternatively, you can whirl the batter in a blender for about 20 seconds.)

2. Place a large (10- or 12-inch) ovenproof skillet over medium-high heat. Add the butter and let it melt, 1 to 2 minutes. When the white foam subsides, add the batter and transfer the pan to the hot oven.

(recipe continues)

3. Bake until the pancake is puffed and dark brown around the edges, 15 to 20 minutes.

4. While the pancake is baking, if you are making the sweet version, prepare the lemon sauce by whisking together the confectioners' sugar and lemon juice in a small bowl until smooth.

5. Using oven mitts (be especially careful of that hot skillet handle), remove the skillet from the oven. Top the Dutch baby with either the lemon sauce or more Parmesan, and serve immediately.

tips & tweaks

● Dutch babies, like soufflés, puff up gloriously but temporarily. So if you're planning to photograph yours, have your smartphone at the ready and ask someone else to take it out of the oven. You'll have about 2 minutes max before it falls.

● For the sweet version, instead of lemon sauce, try:

- Maple syrup
- Chocolate sauce
- Butterscotch Sauce (page 180)
- Your favorite jam
- Whipped cream (untraditional, but come on, it's really good)

Foolproof Baked Oats
with Brown Sugar Glaze

Better than instant and easier than regular oatmeal, baked steel-cut oats with nut butter have a fantastic flavor and protein-powered earthiness. The brown sugar on the top melts into a gorgeous syrup, which make this sugar-cereal amazing.

⅓ cup / 80 grams **almond butter** or another nut butter, your choice

2 tablespoons / 28 grams **unsalted butter,** cut into cubes

1½ cups / 265 grams **steel-cut oats** (don't use rolled oats)

½ teaspoon **ground cinnamon**, ginger, or nutmeg

¼ teaspoon **kosher salt**

¼ cup / 50 grams **light** or **dark brown sugar**

Flaky sea salt (optional)

get it set

Heat the oven to 350°F.

Bring 4½ cups of water to a boil in a saucepan.

Set out all your ingredients.

1. Put the nut butter into a 2-quart casserole dish or a 9-inch baking pan and pour the 4½ cups boiling water over it. Stir until the nut butter mostly dissolves (a few lumps are fine).

2. Place a large skillet over medium heat. Add the butter and let it melt until the white foam subsides, about 1 minute. Add the oats and sauté until they smell nutty, 2 to 4 minutes. Stir in the cinnamon and kosher salt and sauté for another minute. Scrape the oats into the casserole dish and stir well.

3. Cover the casserole dish with foil, put it in the oven, and bake for 30 minutes. Using oven mitts, uncover the dish and give the oats a stir with a long-handled spoon. Cover again and bake until the oats have absorbed all the water, 30 to 40 minutes longer.

4. Remove the casserole dish from the oven and let it rest for 5 minutes before uncovering it. Sprinkle the brown sugar all over the oats (it will melt on contact), then sprinkle lightly with flaky sea salt, if you like. Serve immediately.

tips & tweaks

● How does "peanut butter cup oatmeal" sound? Use peanut butter instead of almond butter, and instead of the brown sugar, sprinkle some mini chocolate chips on top of the oatmeal. Still healthful, very fun.

● To add taste and texture, mix one or more of these into the oats just before serving:

- Dried fruit
- Cubed fresh fruit, especially bananas
- Shredded coconut (sweetened or unsweetened)
- Chopped toasted nuts

Maple Coconut Granola

The maple and coconut make this granola great any way you want to eat it. It's a no-fuss recipe, because you don't need to have every single ingredient on the list—as long as you use most of them, the recipe will still work perfectly. Bonus: You can also add more of the ingredients you really like.

(See Weigh It Up, page 13.)

3 cups / 280 grams **old-fashioned rolled oats** (don't use instant or quick-cooking oats, which are too soft)

1½ cups / 220 grams **raw nuts,** coarsely chopped (pecans, almonds, cashews, walnuts, or pistachios work well, or use a combination)

1 cup / 289 grams **raw pumpkin seeds** or sunflower seeds

1 cup / 45 grams **unsweetened coconut chips** (use the big flakes, not the small shreds)

¾ cup / 225 grams **maple syrup**

½ cup / 105 grams some kind of **oil:** olive, coconut, sunflower, grapeseed, canola

1 teaspoon / 6 grams **kosher salt**

1¼ teaspoons **ground sweet spice,** such as cinnamon, cardamom, or ginger (or a combination)

¾ cup / 115 grams **dried fruit,** such as dried cherries or cut-up apricots (optional)

get it set

SPECIAL EQUIPMENT: A scale is optional but makes this go faster

Heat the oven to 300°F.

Line a rimmed sheet pan with parchment paper or a nonstick liner, or lightly grease it.

Set out all your ingredients.

1. In a large bowl, combine the oats, nuts, pumpkin seeds, coconut chips, maple syrup, oil, salt, and spice(s). Toss everything well with your hands or a rubber spatula. Spread it in an even layer on the sheet pan.

2. Place the sheet pan in the oven and bake for 45 to 55 minutes, stirring every 10 minutes (you can set a second timer if you need a reminder). The granola is done when it's evenly and deeply golden brown all over. If it's too pale, it might not get crunchy; if it gets too dark, it can taste burnt or bitter.

3. Transfer the sheet pan to a wire rack and let the granola cool completely.

4. If you're adding the dried fruit, put it into a large bowl, add the granola, and toss well. Store the granola at room temperature for up to 2 months.

tips & tweaks

● The dried fruit is always added after the granola comes out of the oven so it stays nice and chewy. Baking it would dry it out.

● There are so many ways to tweak granola. As long as you keep the amount of oats, oil, and sweetener the same, you can change up all the other elements. Substitute different nuts or seeds, use whatever dried fruit you like, swap out maple syrup for honey or agave syrup, skip or change up the spices.

Egg Academy
Perfect Every Time

When it comes to cooking eggs, different moods call for different methods. Crack the code (heh heh), and with a little practice your eggs will be perfect every time.

boiled
hard, soft, or jammy

1. Place cold eggs in a medium pot and cover them with cold water.

2. Bring the pot of water to a boil.

3. Remove the pot from the heat, cover it with a lid, and let it stand until the eggs are done to the way you like them (see chart).

4. Transfer the eggs to a bowl of cold water and let them cool for at least 2 minutes before peeling.

5. Peel the boiled eggs: Remove them from the ice water. Gently crack an egg against a hard flat surface, like a counter, then peel off the shell with your fingers. Or gently slide a spoon between the egg and the cracked shell to pry the shell off in large pieces.

cooking times*

6 minutes	soft-boiled (with a very runny yolk)
7 minutes	ramen-style (with a thick but still runny yolk)
8 minutes	jammy (with a moist and vibrant orange yolk)
9 minutes	hard-boiled (with a firm and pale yellow yolk)

*The cooking times are starting points, and can differ quite a lot depending on the egg's initial temperature, its size, the season, and even the altitude, so start with the times listed, and if it's not right, in your next try adjust in 15-second increments up or down depending on how you like it.

scrambled
light and fluffy

1. Crack as many eggs as you'd like into a bowl (figure 2 eggs per serving) and use a fork to beat them until the whites and yolks are just mixed together, but no more (overmixing gives the cooked eggs a spongy texture). Add a pinch of salt and pepper.

2. In a nonstick skillet set over low heat, melt ½ to 1 tablespoon of butter per egg. (You can also substitute olive oil or coconut oil for the butter, each of which will impart its own taste to the eggs.) Slide the eggs into the hot skillet. Using a heatproof rubber spatula (or a fork in a pinch), stir the eggs into large clumps for 1 to 2 minutes. Be sure to scrape the bottom of the skillet occasionally to keep the eggs cooking consistently and to prevent them from burning. Turn off the heat when the eggs are still runny, and let them finish cooking in the warm skillet. It's better to undercook rather than to overcook scrambled eggs, because you can always turn the heat back on. Once they're overcooked, there's no going back.

fried sunny-side up
runny yolk, whites with crispy edges

1. Heat a heavy skillet over medium-high heat. When the pan is hot, add about ½ tablespoon butter per egg. (You can use another type of fat to fry your egg—olive oil, lard, and bacon grease are all delicious.) Let the butter (or whatever fat you're using) coat the pan and heat for 10 seconds.

2. Crack each egg and let it slide from the shell into the pan. Don't crowd the pan—leaving space between eggs lets the whites get crispy. While the eggs cook, carefully tilt the skillet and use a spoon to collect some of the hot fat. Very gently pour the fat onto the whites to help them cook.

3. Turn off the heat as soon as the eggs are done on the edges, place a lid on the skillet, and let it sit for a minute or less. This allows the tops to firm up without overcooking the yolks. The whites should be crisp and golden at the edges and the yolks still runny. Season the eggs with salt and pepper.

fried over easy
runny yolk, whites cooked top and bottom

1. Follow the directions for fried sunny-side up, but in Step 3, turn off the heat just *before* the edges have crisped.

2. Flip the egg by sliding a spatula (the thinner the better) under the egg, and then turning the spatula upside down by rotating your wrist in a quick, steady motion without raising the spatula. Avoid picking up the egg and trying to drop it upside down. The yolk could break if the egg drops from even a few inches, so the key is to keep the spatula close to the pan surface. This takes practice!

3. Turn off the heat and let the second side cook in the warm pan. It will finish cooking faster than the first. To keep the yolk runny, you really just want to cook that last bit of egg white that's on top of the egg, so watch for the right doneness on the edges and then carefully slide the spatula under the egg so as not to break the yolk.

fried

soft and supple without crisping

1. Heat a skillet on medium-low heat and melt ½ tablespoon butter per egg in the pan.

2. Crack the egg into the pan and cover the pan with a lid. Let the egg cook, undisturbed, for 2 to 4 minutes, until the white is cooked through and the yolk is still runny.

poached

firm whites, runny yolk

1. Crack each egg into its own cup or ramekin.

2. Bring a few inches of water to a gentle simmer in a saucepan, or if you are cooking more than a few eggs, in a skillet.

3. When the water is barely simmering, slip the eggs, one at a time, into the water.

4. Stir the water gently in a circle around each egg, without disturbing the egg, to create a whirlpool. This will keep the egg white from spreading out like a ghostly spider.

5. Cover the pan with a lid and turn off the heat. Let it sit for 4 minutes. If the whites aren't set yet, re-cover and let the eggs continue to cook off the heat, checking them every 20 seconds.

6. Use a slotted spoon to scoop out the eggs one by one. To eliminate dripping water, pat the bottom of the spoon on a clean kitchen towel after picking up each egg.

baked

firm, consistent whites, runny yolk

1. Heat the oven to 400°F. Brush 6-ounce ramekins, or other small ovenproof ceramic bowls or cups, with butter or olive oil and place them on a rimmed sheet pan.

2. Crack an egg or two into each ramekin. Sprinkle with salt and pepper and bake until the egg whites are just set and the yolks are still jiggly, 10 to 15 minutes. The eggs will continue to cook once they're out of the oven, so it's okay if the center looks underdone. The parts of the egg that touch the sides of the ramekin will cook faster than the center.

3. Remove the ramekins from the oven and let them cool slightly before serving.

Buttermilk Bliss Pancakes

SERVES 4

A pancake at its best is basically a syrup sponge. For this it needs maximum fluffiness: the more air pockets, the more syrup it holds. The right amount of baking powder and some judicious whisking will give you maximum air pockets, making these pancakes light, fluffy, and ready to hold tons of syrup.

(See Weigh It Up, page 13.)

2 cups / 250 grams **all-purpose flour**

2 teaspoons / 8 grams **baking powder**

1 teaspoon / 5 grams **baking soda**

1 teaspoon / 6 grams **kosher salt**

2 large **eggs**, lightly beaten

1 tablespoon **honey** (21 grams) or sugar (12 grams)

2¼ cups / 540 grams **buttermilk** (see Tips & Tweaks, page 35)

3 tablespoons / 42 grams **unsalted butter**, melted, plus more for frying

1 teaspoon / 5 grams **vanilla extract**

Grapeseed, sunflower, or **canola oil,** for frying

Maple syrup or other toppings (see Tips & Tweaks, page 35), for serving

get it set

Heat the oven to 300°F to keep the pancakes warm until you're done frying them all (or else serve them as they come out of the pan).

Put serving plates or a platter or sheet pan next to the stove to hold the just-cooked pancakes.

Set out all your ingredients.

1. In a large bowl, whisk together the flour, baking powder, baking soda, and salt until everything is well combined.

2. In a separate bowl, whisk together the eggs and honey until the egg whites and yolks are well combined. Whisk in the buttermilk, melted butter, and vanilla. Pour the buttermilk mixture into the flour mixture and stir until just combined. Let the mixture sit for at least 10 minutes before frying (see Tips & Tweaks, page 35).

3. Heat a skillet or griddle over medium-high heat for 20 seconds. Add a drizzle of oil to the pan, then a little butter, and let the butter melt into the oil. When the foam from the butter subsides (about 1 minute), pour ¼-cup dollops of batter into the pan

(recipe continues)

to form pancakes, leaving space around each. Cook the pancakes until bubbles form on the surface without bursting and the edges begin to set, 2 to 3 minutes. Flip the pancakes over and cook until golden on the second side, 1 to 2 minutes more. As they are cooked, transfer the pancakes to plates and serve immediately, or put them on an ovenproof platter or sheet pan and leave in the 300°F oven to keep warm.

4. Cook additional pancakes, adding more oil and butter to the skillet as needed. Serve the pancakes hot, topped with syrup or other toppings.

tips & tweaks

● The secret to the fluffiest pancakes is letting the batter sit for at least 10 minutes so the flour can absorb all the liquid. Don't rush it!

● The buttermilk has lactic acid that reacts with the baking soda to produce carbon dioxide, which helps make these pancakes rise. But if you don't have buttermilk, you can replace the lactic acid with another acid by spiking the same amount of regular whole milk with 2 tablespoons lemon juice or white vinegar.

● Or, to use yogurt (which also has lactic acid), thin it down with a little milk so it's pourable: For regular yogurt, use about 2 cups yogurt plus ¼ cup milk; for Greek yogurt (or sour cream), use 1¾ cups yogurt and ½ cup milk.

● Combining a bit of oil with the butter to fry the pancakes keeps the butter from burning in the pan.

● For whole-grain pancakes, substitute 1 cup mixed whole-grain flours (some combination of whole-wheat, spelt, buckwheat, rye, and rolled oats) for 1 cup of all-purpose flour.

● If your pancake wants to be more than just a syrup sponge, try an add-in. The key to add-ins is not to overdo it: A tablespoon or two per pancake goes a long way. Let the pancake cook on one side, then sprinkle in your add-in just before it's time to flip it.

- Blueberries
- Sliced strawberries
- Chocolate chips
- Dried cherries
- Sliced bananas
- Peaches
- (I could go on, but you get the idea.)

Fresh Custardy French Toast

In the olden days, "French" toast was a way to use leftover stale bread—although the practice is older than France itself, going at least as far back as ancient Rome. In the twenty-first century, toasted bread gives you the same custardy perfection. Brioche and challah (page 227) are ideal for French toast, since their egg-based doughs match up with the egg batter, but most breads without nuts or seeds will work great.

6 to 8 (1-inch-thick) slices **challah, brioche**, or **soft white sandwich bread**, fresh or stale

5 large **eggs**

2 large **egg yolks** (see How to Separate Eggs, opposite page)

1 cup / 240 grams **whole milk** (nondairy is fine)

½ cup / 120 grams **heavy cream** or **coconut milk**

2 tablespoons / 40 grams **honey**, maple syrup, or agave syrup, plus more for serving

1 teaspoon / 5 grams **vanilla extract** or **ground cinnamon**

½ teaspoon finely grated **lemon zest** (optional)

Pinch of **kosher salt**

4 to 6 tablespoons / 57 to 85 grams **unsalted butter**

get it set

Set out all your ingredients.

Heat the oven to 375°F (if using fresh bread).

1. Arrange the bread slices on a sheet pan. Bake until lightly golden in spots, 3 to 7 minutes. Transfer pan to a rack to cool. If you're making a smaller batch of French toast, toast the bread in your toaster. (If using stale bread, skip this step.)

2. Set oven temperature to 250°F if you want to keep the French toast warm (otherwise, serve slices as they cook).

3. In a large bowl, whisk the eggs and egg yolks until the whites and yolks are well mixed together. Whisk in the milk, cream, honey, vanilla, lemon zest if using, and salt.

4. Working with one slice at a time, add the bread to the egg mixture and push it down to submerge it. Let it soak for a few minutes, then turn it over carefully, so it doesn't break. Allow it to soak until it's saturated. When you squeeze it gently, liquid should bubble out.

5. Transfer the slices to the sheet pan that you toasted them on, and let sit at room

temperature for 5 minutes to firm them up, which helps them brown when frying them.

6. Place a large skillet over medium-high heat. Add 2 tablespoons of the butter and let it melt. After it melts, let it continue to cook for another minute or two, until you can smell the butter turning nutty and see the white foam settle to the bottom of the pan and turn golden brown. (This is called brown butter, and it adds a ton of flavor.)

7. Immediately add 2 or 3 bread slices to the pan. They should fit in one layer without overlapping. Cook the bread on one side until it turns golden brown, 2 to 3 minutes, then flip and cook the other side, another 3 minutes. Serve the slices immediately, or transfer them to an ovenproof serving platter or a clean sheet pan and put them in the oven to stay warm.

8. Continue frying the French toast, browning more butter in the pan between batches, until it's all cooked. Serve hot or warm, with syrup on top.

tips & tweaks

● If you're listening for it, you can actually *hear* the butter brown. After it melts, it will sizzle for a minute or two, then go really quiet. That's when you should start watching it. When the white foam (from the milk solids) turns light brown, it's done.

● To make an almond version, substitute ¼ teaspoon almond extract for the vanilla. Or if you're using coconut milk, you can use ½ teaspoon coconut extract.

how to separate eggs

There are lots of ways to separate an egg, but my favorite is the hand-to-hand version. Always use eggs straight from the fridge; cold yolks are firmer and less fragile than room-temperature ones.

1. Wash your hands well. Have two small bowls (or containers) ready.

2. Working over one of the bowls, crack an egg on the counter, then open it into your hand (this is kind of gross, but mostly cool). Catch the yolk in your palm while you let the white ooze between your fingers and into the bowl.

3. Slide the yolk gently into the second bowl.

4. Repeat. If any shell gets into the bowls, use a larger piece of shell to scoop it out.

5. Wash your hands well again.

The whites will keep for 2 weeks in a covered container in the fridge or up to 6 months in the freezer. The yolks will keep for 5 days in the fridge and up to 4 months in the freezer.

Hot Honey Butter Popovers

Crispy edges, fluffy centers, and a mandatory slather of butter—spiked with honey and spices—might make these popovers the coziest weekend breakfast there is. (Watch your back, French toast.) Time the baking carefully: Popovers can get gummy if they're allowed to cool, so serve them hot, hot, hot from the oven.

(See Weigh It Up, page 13.)

1 cup / 240 grams **whole milk** (nondairy is fine), at room temperature

3 large **eggs**, at room temperature

2 tablespoons / 28 grams **unsalted butter**, melted, plus more butter for the pans (or use nonstick cooking spray)

1 teaspoon / 4 grams **sugar**

½ teaspoon **fine sea salt**

1 cup / 125 grams **all-purpose flour**

honey butter

½ cup / 113 grams **butter**, preferably salted, at room temperature

2 tablespoons / 40 grams **honey**

¼ teaspoon **ground cardamom** or **cinnamon** (optional)

Pinch of **kosher salt** (if using unsalted butter)

get it set

SPECIAL EQUIPMENT: Popover pan or a muffin tin, cups brushed with butter or coated with cooking spray

Take the eggs, milk, and butter out of the fridge 30 to 60 minutes ahead to let them come to room temperature. (See When Not to Be Chill, page 255.)

Set out all your ingredients.

Heat the oven to 450°F.

1. In a large measuring cup with a spout (this will make pouring easier later) or in a bowl, whisk together the milk, eggs, butter, sugar, and sea salt until frothy. Add the flour and whisk until the batter is mostly smooth, though it's fine if a few clumps remain. Or, if you're using a blender, you can put everything in at the same time and whizz the ingredients until smooth.

2. Pour the batter into the prepared cups, filling them about two-thirds of the way in the popover pan or three-quarters of the way in the muffin tin. Bake for 20 minutes.

3. **Meanwhile, make the honey butter:** Put the butter in a bowl and use a fork to smash it up. (The softer it is, the easier this is.) Stir in the honey, spice if you like, and kosher salt if you're using unsalted butter. Set the honey butter aside at room temperature for serving. (Leftovers can be kept in the fridge for up to 2 weeks.)

4. When the popovers have cooked for 20 minutes, reduce the heat to 350°F. **If you're using a popover pan,** bake the popovers for another 20 minutes, until golden brown and puffed. **If you're using a muffin tin,** bake them for another 10 minutes. Keep tabs on this by looking through the window in the oven door. Do not open the oven door until the last 5 minutes of baking or the popovers won't puff. Serve them as hot as you can stand it, slathered with the honey butter. You won't have to wait long–they cool fast.

tips & tweaks

● Keep the oven door closed during baking until the very end or the popovers won't rise to their puffiest potential. Use your oven light and the window to peek in on their progress.

● A popover tin, which has deeper cups than a muffin pan, is specially designed to give you the highest and most dramatic rise (the batter literally pops over the tops of the cups as it bakes). But muffin tins work just fine.

● You can make the batter a few hours or even the night before; just store it in the fridge until it's time to cook. Give it a quick whisk to redistribute the ingredients before pouring it into the pans for baking.

● Instead of adding the optional spice to the honey butter, you can add a teaspoon of vanilla extract or a few drops of almond extract.

OMG, I Smell Bacon!

SERVES 6 TO 8

The aroma of bacon has been known to alter lives, change the course of history, and at times even draw sleepy people out of cozy beds. The plain classic version is good enough for most of us, of course, but for a nice bacon boost, try adding a little brown sugar and mustard. Baking it in the oven is the easiest and least messy way to cook bacon, and just as good-smelling.

1 pound **bacon** (pork, turkey, or duck), sliced thick or thin

¼ cup **light** or **dark brown sugar** (optional)

Mustard or **hot sauce**, such as Sriracha or Tabasco, for brushing (optional)

get it set

Set out all your ingredients.

Line 1 or 2 rimmed sheet pans with parchment paper or foil to make cleanup easier (optional but helpful).

Put a plate lined with a paper towel next to the oven to absorb the grease from the cooked bacon. This will help keep the bacon crispy.

1. Arrange the bacon on the sheet pan, leaving space between the strips. If your bacon is thick, you might be able to fit it all on one sheet pan. Thinner-cut bacon will have more strips per pound, and you may need two sheet pans.

2. For non-spicy candied bacon, sprinkle the brown sugar evenly over the bacon strips. If you want it spicy-sweet, brush the bacon very lightly with mustard or hot sauce before sprinkling on the brown sugar. Otherwise leave the bacon plain.

3. Put the sheet pan(s) in the oven and then set the heat for 350°F. Starting in a cold oven helps the bacon bake evenly, without hot spots, and you won't have to flip it.

4. Start checking the bacon after 12 minutes for thin slices; it will probably take more like 15 minutes, and up to 30 for thicker slices. It's done when it's golden to medium brown, depending on how crisp you like your bacon. The darker it is, the crispier it will be (but don't let it get really dark brown, or it will taste burnt).

5. Using oven mitts, remove the pan(s) from the oven. Be very careful not to slosh the bacon grease. Use tongs to transfer the bacon strips to the waiting paper towel–lined plate. The bacon will crisp up as it cools slightly, so it's best eaten 5 or 10 minutes after cooking.

tips & tweaks

● If you're using the brown sugar and mustard option, wake it up even more by adding spices to the brown sugar before sprinkling it on the bacon. A pinch or two of cinnamon or ginger makes it even sweeter; cumin, coriander, black pepper, or curry powder makes it more savory.

Morning Fruit Smoothie

You can put almost any fruit into a smoothie, but I find the most satisfying ones have a harmonic balance of ingredients. Start with any fruit you like, maybe mixing tangy citrus with sweet berries, and make sure to add a banana for a creamy texture. Adding nut butter gives the mix a jolt of protein and makes it richer, and you can sneak in some greens to give it an earthy note and make it even more healthful.

½ to 1 cup **milk** (regular, almond, coconut, any kind works here—even buttermilk for a tangy smoothie) or coconut water

2 cups **cut-up fruit** (fresh or frozen), any kind

1 ripe **banana**

Optional (add any or all of the following): 1 or 2 **pitted dates**, 2 tablespoons **peanut** or **almond butter**, a squirt of **honey**, ½ cup **tender greens** like spinach or baby kale

get it set

Set out all your ingredients.

1. Put everything into a blender, starting with ½ cup liquid (milk or coconut water). Blend at high speed until smooth, then blend in more liquid if it's too thick.

2. Pour into two glasses and drink immediately. Smoothies can separate and turn grainy if left to sit for more than a few minutes.

tips & tweaks

● Use a combination of fresh and frozen fruit for a cold and refreshing smoothie. If you don't have any frozen fruit, you can toss an ice cube or two into the blender to chill things down.

● This recipe loves being tweaked— that's the beauty of a smoothie. Once you have a banana, your anchor fruit, you can throw in:

• Berries
• Cubed melon
• Pineapple
• Sliced apple

• Frozen mango chunks
• You tell me

fruit you have

a perfectly balanced smoothie

fruit you like

Sandwiches

Double Melt Grilled Cheese

You don't grill a grilled cheese sandwich, you *fry* it—until it's crispy, golden, and melty-centered. The secret to getting that crispiness is to coat the bread on both sides with softened butter or mayonnaise, which also softens and flavors the cheese filling. Why two different cheeses? Use cheddar for richness and Monterey Jack for gooeyness. Or feel free to use all cheddar or American cheese.

2 slices **white or whole-wheat sandwich bread**

About 2 tablespoons **unsalted butter**, at room temperature, or mayonnaise

1 to 2 teaspoons **condiment of choice** (optional; see Tips & Tweaks)

2 tablespoons / 15 grams shredded **sharp cheddar cheese**

2 tablespoons / 15 grams shredded **Monterey Jack cheese**

get it set

Put a cutting board next to the stove.

If you're using butter, take it out of the fridge 30 to 60 minutes ahead to allow it to come to room temperature. (See When Not to Be Chill, page 255.)

Set out all your ingredients.

1. Spread one side of both bread slices with butter or mayonnaise. If you are using a condiment, spread it over the butter or mayo on one of the slices. Put the cheeses on top. Cover with the other bread slice, butter- or mayo-side down, to make a sandwich.

2. Spread butter or mayo on both outside surfaces of the sandwich. It's easiest to use a spatula from this point on, we have a very slippery sandwich here.

3. Put a skillet over medium heat and let it heat for 30 seconds. Add the sandwich. Fry until the bread is golden on the bottom, about 2 minutes. Use a spatula to flip the sandwich and fry on the other side, pressing down on it once or twice with the spatula, until golden, 2 to 3 minutes.

4. Transfer the sandwich to the cutting board. Cut the sandwich in half diagonally. Serve while it's still crispy, melty, and warm.

tips & tweaks

● Zip up your grilled cheese by adding condiments before frying. Or serve any of these on the side, for dunking.

- Mango chutney
- Miso paste
- Sriracha
- Tabasco
- Whole-grain Dijon mustard
- Harissa
- Pickle relish
- Marmalade
- Any spicy South Asian pickle, such as Indian lime pickle
- Ketchup (why not?)

Chip-Crisp Quesadillas
with Pickled Jalapeños

I was making quesadillas one day, when some of the cheese leaked out onto the skillet and turned brown and potato-chip crisp. My daughter, Dahlia, and I went nuts for the delicate crunch. Now I re-create this on purpose by squishing the tortillas with a spatula as they cook. The soft gooey cheese in the center, the crispy cheese at the edges, and the pickled jalapeños give this quesadilla a nacho crunch without the chips!

pickled jalapeños

- 1 **jalapeño**, seeded if desired and thinly sliced crosswise (see Chile Pepper Alert, page 193)

- 3 tablespoons **cider vinegar**, white wine vinegar, or fresh lime juice

- ½ teaspoon **sugar**

- Pinch of **coarse kosher salt**

quesadilla

- 1 teaspoon **olive oil**

- 2 (8-inch) **corn** or **flour tortillas**

- ½ cup (about 2 ounces / 60 grams) shredded **Monterey Jack** or **pepper Jack cheese**

- **Sour cream,** for serving (optional)

- **Salsa,** store-bought or homemade (see Chunky Cherry Tomato Salsa, page 61), for serving (optional)

2. Make the quesadilla: Place a nonstick skillet over medium heat, then add the oil and let it heat up for about 10 seconds.

3. Add one tortilla to the pan, then sprinkle the cheese evenly over its surface, all the way to the edges but no farther. Top with the remaining tortilla and let it cook for 1 minute to start melting the cheese. Use a spatula to press down on the quesadilla. Some of the cheese should ooze out. Let it bubble and brown, creating lacy crisp edges, but don't let it burn. Flip the quesadilla and let it cook for 2 minutes on the other side, until the quesadilla is hot and the cheese has melted.

4. Transfer the quesadilla to the cutting board. Cut it into triangles and serve with the pickled jalapeños, sour cream and salsa, if you like.

get it set

Put a cutting board next to the stove.

Set out all your ingredients.

1. Pickle the jalapeños: Put the jalapeños in a small bowl and stir in the vinegar, sugar, and salt. Let sit at room temperature for at least 1 hour. Store in the refrigerator for up to 1 week.

tips & tweaks

● Skip the pickled jalapeños and serve with guacamole (homemade, see page 63, or store-bought) on the side.

● Not a Monterey Jack fan? Cheddar or Gouda also make terrific quesadilla fillings.

The Big BLAT

The BLT is a diner classic, all about the interplay of crispy bacon with soft lettuce and juicy, sweet tomatoes. But add avocado slices and you have a BLAT, making it more plush when you bite into it. Mixing the mayonnaise with olive oil (a BLOOAT?) and mustard (BLAMT!) or hot sauce (have a BLAHST) makes it taste a little brighter, but you can skip that step if you like your mayonnaise on the sweeter side, or if you favor shorter acronyms.

3 strips **thick-cut bacon**

1 small **tomato,** sliced thin

2 to 4 **avocado slices**

Kosher salt and **freshly ground black pepper,** for sprinkling

Fresh lemon or **lime juice,** for sprinkling

2 tablespoons **mayonnaise**

1 teaspoon **extra-virgin olive oil** (optional)

½ teaspoon **Dijon mustard** or a dash of hot sauce (optional)

2 slices **bread** (any kind you like, but soft sandwich bread or challah is really nice here)

Romaine or other lettuce leaves

get it set

Put a plate lined with a paper towel next to the oven to absorb the grease from the cooked bacon. This will help keep the bacon crispy.

Line a rimmed sheet pan with parchment paper or foil for easier cleanup (optional but helpful).

Set out all your ingredients.

1. Arrange the bacon on the sheet pan, leaving space between the strips. Put the pan in the oven and then set the heat for 350°F. (Starting in a cold oven helps the bacon cook evenly, without hot spots, and you won't have to flip it.) Bake for 15 to 25 minutes. It's done when it's golden to medium brown, depending on how crisp you like your bacon. The darker it is, the crispier it will be (but don't let it get really dark brown, or it will taste burnt).

2. Using oven mitts, remove the pan from the oven. Move slowly and be very careful not to slosh the bacon grease. Use tongs to transfer the bacon strips to the waiting paper towel–lined plate.

(recipe continues)

3. While the bacon is cooking, put the tomato and avocado slices on a plate and sprinkle lightly with salt, pepper, and lemon juice. Let sit for 5 to 10 minutes to dissolve the salt. (This helps the tomato and avocado absorb some of the seasonings.)

4. Put the mayonnaise in a small bowl, and mix in the olive oil and mustard or hot sauce if using.

5. When the bacon comes out of the oven, toast the bread in your toaster. While the toast is still warm, spread one side of each slice with the mayonnaise and put the slices, mayo-side up, on a cutting board. Put the tomatoes on one piece of toast and top with the bacon, avocado, and then the lettuce. Cover with the other toast slice, mayo-side down. Press to close, and use a serrated knife to cut the sandwich in half. Eat it immediately, preferably while the toast and bacon are still a little warm.

tips & tweaks

● You can leave off the avocado for a classic BLT.

● Thin slices of red or sweet white onion are excellent on a BLAT, a BLT, a BLOOAT, or indeed, a BLAMT. (See Onion Prep, page 12.)

● For a BLAT blast, zip up the mayonnaise even more by adding a pinch of ground cumin or coriander, or a teaspoon of chopped kimchi, pickled jalapeños (store-bought or see page 48), or sauerkraut.

Fried PB & Banana

This PB&B is one of those crispy, soft-centered flavor bombs that can happen when you fry a sandwich. The peanut butter, honey, and banana get runny and soft in the center, while the bread gets crisp and browned. Use soft white or whole-wheat sandwich bread for this dish, not a hard-crusted bread.

½ ripe **banana,** peeled

2 slices **white** or **whole-wheat sandwich bread**

2 tablespoons **peanut butter** (crunchy or smooth)

Fine sea salt, for sprinkling (optional)

Honey, for drizzling

½ tablespoon **unsalted butter**

get it set

Put a cutting board next to the stove.

Set out all your ingredients.

1. Cut the banana lengthwise into 4 slices. Spread one side of each slice of bread with the peanut butter. If your peanut butter is unsalted, you can sprinkle a little salt on top of it to bring out the flavors. Unsalted peanut butter can taste flat.

2. Lay the banana slices on top of the peanut butter on one slice, then drizzle the bananas with a little honey. Top with the other bread slice, peanut butter–side down.

3. Put a skillet over medium heat and add the butter. When it melts, add the sandwich to the pan and fry it until it's golden brown on the bottom, 2 to 3 minutes. Use a spatula to flip the sandwich and cook, pressing down on it once or twice with the spatula to keep the bread in contact with the hot pan, until that side is golden, 2 to 3 minutes.

4. Transfer the sandwich to the cutting board. Using a serrated knife, cut the sandwich in half diagonally, and serve immediately.

Crushing It!
Avocado Toast

Avocado toast seems like a no-brainer, but it lives and dies by the details. The bread should be hearty and flavorful, and you want ripe, velvety avocados, seasoned with enough salt and acid to make the flavor come alive. You can step it up with garnishes like herbs, onions, or seeds. Personalize it with your favorite or invent your own combinations.

2 thick slices **crusty bread** (see Tips & Tweaks)

1 **garlic clove,** halved crosswise

Extra-virgin olive oil, for drizzling

1 perfectly ripe **avocado** (see Tips & Tweaks)

Fine sea salt and **freshly ground black pepper**

Fresh lemon or **lime juice** to taste (or use a mild vinegar like cider, sherry, rice, or balsamic)

garnishes
(choose one or a few)

Chopped or torn **fresh soft herbs,** like basil, mint, cilantro, or parsley

Baby arugula or **spinach**

Thinly sliced **jalapeño** or other chile pepper, seeded or not (see Chile Pepper Alert, page 193)

Thinly sliced **red** or **sweet white onion,** or pickled onions (see Veggie Quick Pickles, page 67)

Poached or **fried egg** (see Egg Academy, page 30)

Everything bagel seasoning

Sesame seeds or **pumpkin seeds** (also called pepitas)

get it set

Set out all your ingredients.

1. Toast the bread. When the toast is cool enough to handle but still warm, rub the cut side of one of the garlic halves all over both sides of one slice, and repeat with the remaining piece of garlic and the other slice of toast. Drizzle the top of each toast slice with a little olive oil.

2. Halve the avocado and take out the pit. Use a wide spoon (a soupspoon is good) to scoop out the flesh from the skin and plop it directly onto the toast slices. Use a fork to mash the avocado into the bread, leaving as many large chunks as possible. The object here isn't to make an avocado puree, but to break up the avocado flesh somewhat so it can accept the seasonings, and to get it to adhere to the toast so it doesn't fall off when you pick it up.

3. Season the avocado generously with salt and pepper, and sprinkle with lemon juice. Drizzle with a little more olive oil, then top with whatever garnishes you like, or leave it plain for a minimalist toast.

tips & tweaks

● The soul of avocado toast is a perfectly ripe avocado. Always buy rock-hard avocados and let them ripen on your counter, even if it takes a few days. The soft avocados in the supermarket are often bruised on the inside from too much squeezing; when you cut them open, you'll see brown patches. Better to ripen your own in a spot where you know they won't be jostled too much.

Snack Like You Mean It

Crunchy Snack Crackeritos

This is one of those bet-you-can't-stop snacks, and it's super easy to make. Just pick a spice mix and go to town. There's Italian cheesy, spicy nooch, crunchy bagel, and even a sweet cinnamon version, depending on whether you crave savory or sweet.

2 cups **any crackers,** like saltines, Ritz Crackers, Wheat Thins, or Triscuits (gluten-free crackers work here, too!)

⅓ cup **extra-virgin olive oil**

seasoning mixes

Parmesan
6 tablespoons / 40 grams **grated Parmesan cheese,** 1 teaspoon **dried oregano,** 1 teaspoon **garlic powder,** and ¼ teaspoon **crushed red pepper flakes**

Nooch
1 tablespoon **nutritional yeast,** ½ teaspoon **onion powder,** ¼ teaspoon **paprika,** and a pinch of **salt**

Everything Bagel
4 tablespoons **Everything Bagel Seasoning** and a pinch of **salt**

Cinnamon Sugar
2 tablespoons granulated **sugar** and 1 teaspoon **ground cinnamon**

get it set

Heat the oven to 300°F.

Set out all your ingredients.

1. In a large mixing bowl, toss together the crackers and oil. Add the seasoning mix, and with your hands, gently toss everything until the crackers are evenly coated.

2. Arrange the crackers in one layer on a large rimmed sheet pan. Bake until golden, 10 to 15 minutes.

3. Transfer the sheet pan to a wire rack and let the crackers cool completely, about 30 minutes. The crackers can be stored in a ziplock bag or other airtight container for 1 week.

Yes to That Parmesan Crisps

Cheesy? Yep. Crunchy? Oh yes. Yum factor? Off the charts. These cheesy, crunchy crisps are great eaten out of hand or coarsely crumbled over salads as croutons. Don't let the simple recipe fool you—they have a deep, rich flavor. But, yeah, they're ridiculously easy to make.

2 cups / 7 ounces / 200 grams **coarsely shredded Parmesan cheese**

1 teaspoon **fresh** or **dried thyme leaves** or chopped fresh rosemary leaves

get it set

Heat the oven to 375°F.

Line a rimmed sheet pan with a nonstick liner or parchment paper.

Set out all your ingredients.

1. Dump the cheese into the center of the sheet pan and use your hands to spread it out into one thin, even layer (a few gaps are okay). It may not fill the sheet pan and that is fine. Scatter the herbs over the top.

2. Bake until the cheese is melted and golden, 7 to 12 minutes. Transfer the pan to a wire rack to cool completely. When it is cool, break the crispy cheese into pieces for snacking.

tips & tweaks

- Don't use finely grated, powdery Parmesan here (we're not even gonna talk about the stuff in the can). You want the texture from the large shards of cheese. Buy it shredded in large pieces, or grate a chunk of it yourself on the large holes of a grater.

- These keep for up to a week, stored in an airtight container at room temperature.

- Skip the herbs and sprinkle the cheese with black pepper. Or to give the crackers extra zip, try spices like cumin or curry powder.

Chunky Cherry Tomato Salsa

MAKES 1 CUP

Sometimes all you need to do to get the most flavor out of an ingredient is to dice it. The big flavor in this salsa comes from the small effort of cutting up cherry tomatoes, which are great from a summer garden or the farmers' market, and are even very good from the supermarket all year round.

1 cup (8 ounces) diced **cherry tomatoes** (¼-inch pieces)

1 tablespoon chopped **red onion** (see Onion Prep, page 12)

1 teaspoon seeded and minced **jalapeño** (see Chile Pepper Alert, page 193), or more (optional) to taste

1 teaspoon **fresh lime juice**, or more to taste

1½ tablespoons finely chopped **fresh cilantro**

½ teaspoon **kosher salt**, or more to taste

get it set

Set out all your ingredients.

1. In a medium bowl, toss the tomatoes, onion, and jalapeño with the lime juice, cilantro, and salt. Let the salsa sit for at least 15 minutes before serving, to develop its flavor.

2. Taste the salsa, and add more salt, jalapeño, and/or lime juice if needed.

tips & tweaks

● Instead of fresh jalapeño, substitute chopped pickled jalapeño (store-bought or see page 48). It gives the salsa a tangier flavor. Or use both!

● Salsa was made for chips, but it's also terrific with other dishes like Chicken Enchiladas (page 206) or mixed into the Cheesy Skillet Black Beans (page 199).

The. Last. Guacamole. Recipe. Ever.

The star of guacamole is obviously the avocado, so keep it in the spotlight. The less you do with it, the better it tastes. This recipe for a classic guac definitely keeps things real, using just a few ingredients for maximum impact. Add more jalapeño if you like it hot, or none at all to keep it mild. Even if it's your first time making guacamole, this could be the last guac recipe you'll ever need.

2 ripe **avocados,** halved and pitted (see Tip and Tweaks, page 55)

¾ teaspoon **kosher salt,** plus more to taste

2 teaspoons **fresh lime juice,** plus more to taste

2 tablespoons finely chopped **fresh cilantro**

1 **scallion** (white and green parts), minced, or 1 tablespoon minced red onion

½ to 1 **jalapeño,** seeds and veins removed (see Chile Pepper Alert, page 193), minced (optional)

Few drops **hot sauce** (optional)

get it set

Set out all your ingredients.

1. Using a spoon, scoop the avocado flesh into a bowl. Add the salt, lime juice, cilantro, scallion, and jalapeño and hot sauce if using. Mash with a fork, leaving the mixture a little chunky.

2. Taste and correct the seasonings, adding more salt and/or lime juice as needed.

tips & tweaks

● This is perfect with tortilla chips (obviously), but it's also a great dip with celery sticks, carrots, tortillas, crackers, or anything else you like to dip.

Lemon Squeezy Greek Yogurt Dip

This recipe needs you to know it is *there* for your dipping, for your dunking, and for your saucing. Dip a veggie, dunk some bread, sauce some meatballs, spread it on a burger. The citrus brings other flavors to life, so this easy dip is basically everybody's BFF.

1½ cups **plain yogurt** (regular or Greek, preferably whole milk) or sour cream

⅔ cup / 3 ounces / 85 grams crumbled **feta cheese** or firm goat cheese

2 tablespoons chopped **fresh dill** or another soft herb, plus more for garnish

1½ teaspoons grated **lemon zest**

1 **garlic clove**, grated, pressed, or minced (see Garlic Prep, page 13)

1 or 2 pinches of **fine sea salt**

Extra-virgin olive oil, for drizzling

Crackers, chunks of bread, cherry tomatoes, sliced cucumbers, carrots, fennel, cauliflower, radishes, zucchini (etc. . . .), for dipping

get it set

Set out all your ingredients.

1. In a mixing bowl, combine the yogurt and cheese, using a fork to mix and mash them together. The cheese should stay pretty chunky at this point.

2. Add the dill, lemon zest, garlic, and a small pinch of salt to the bowl and mix really well; you want the seasonings to distribute into the yogurt, and the cheese to break down a little more (though it should still be somewhat chunky). Taste, and add another pinch of salt if it's needed.

3. To serve, spoon the dip into a shallow bowl and drizzle it with olive oil (be generous!). Scatter more herbs on top and serve with crackers, bread, and/or sliced veggies for dipping.

tips & tweaks

● You can make this a day ahead and store it, covered, in the fridge.

● Feta is saltier and tangier than goat cheese, which is milder, creamier, and a little bit funky tasting (in a good way). Because of the different salt contents in the two cheeses, be sure to taste the dip before you finish seasoning it.

● Skip the cheese and add an extra pinch or two of salt instead—less pungent, just as delicious.

Veggie Quick Pickles

SERVES 6 / MAKES 2 CUPS

Veggie pickles come in all shapes and colors, and each one is different. They're great as a sandwich topping or as a garnish for salads and grain bowls. Or put them all together in a bowl for a bright, pickle-y party snack.

2 cups thinly sliced **crisp vegetables** (cucumbers, onions, fennel, carrots, radishes, or a combination, peeled if you like)

Kosher salt to taste

Granulated sugar to taste

1 tablespoon **fresh lime** or **lemon juice**, or rice or cider vinegar, plus more as needed

1. In a bowl, toss the veggies with a large pinch each of salt and sugar and the lime juice. Let sit for 30 minutes.

2. Taste, and add more salt, sugar, or acid (vinegar or citrus juice) if needed. Use right away or store in the fridge for up to 2 weeks.

pickle-worthy

- Cider vinegar
- White wine vinegar
- Rice vinegar
- White balsamic
- Sherry vinegar

not pickle-worthy

- Distilled white vinegar (too sharp, will make you cough when you eat the pickles)
- Red balsamic vinegar (too dark)

tips & tweaks

● The acid in the vinegar or citrus is what turns vegetables into pickles, softening them and giving them their tanginess. You need a mild vinegar here. Stick to a light-colored vinegar so the pickles will look bright.

● To make pickled chiles, use jalapeños or other fresh chiles.

● To make these spicy, add a pinch of cayenne pepper or chile powder, some sliced jalapeños, or a tablespoon or two of minced kimchi.

Granola Bar Remix,

feat. Cranberry and Ginger

Nutty, crunchy granola bars are fun to make, and they have so much more flavor than the ones from the store. Cranberries and ginger guest-star in this version, balancing out the earthiness of the nuts and seeds. But you can change up the fruit and flavorings to suit yourself (see Tips & Tweaks).

Nonstick cooking spray, preferably coconut oil spray

2 cups **old-fashioned rolled oats**

½ cup **whole raw almonds**

½ cup (packed) **light brown sugar**

3 large **egg whites** (see How to Separate Eggs, page 37)

⅓ cup **grapeseed, sunflower,** or **coconut oil**

¼ teaspoon **almond extract**

½ teaspoon **fine sea salt**

½ teaspoon **ground cinnamon**

¼ teaspoon **ground ginger**

⅓ cup **dried cranberries**

1 tablespoon minced **candied ginger**

½ cup **raw pumpkin seeds** (also called pepitas)

½ cup **raw sunflower seeds**

½ cup **unsweetened flaked coconut**

2 tablespoons **sesame seeds**

get it set

Heat the oven to 300°F.

Line a 9 x 13-inch baking pan with a piece of parchment paper that's long enough to allow 2 inches of overhang on both sides of the pan. Coat the paper lightly with nonstick cooking spray.

Set out all your ingredients.

1. In a food processor, pulse ½ cup of the oats until they're finely ground, about 30 seconds. Dump the ground oats into a small bowl. Add the almonds to the food processor and pulse until finely chopped, 8 to 10 pulses. Add the almonds to the ground oats in the bowl.

2. In a large bowl, whisk the brown sugar, egg whites, oil, almond extract, salt, cinnamon, and ground ginger until well combined. Add the ground oats and almonds, the remaining 1½ cups oats, and the dried cranberries, candied ginger, pepitas, sunflower seeds, coconut flakes, and sesame seeds. Using a rubber spatula, toss until well combined and starting to stick together (the mixture will be sticky).

(recipe continues)

3. Scrape the oat mixture into the prepared baking pan. Lightly coat a large spatula or your hands with nonstick spray and firmly press the mixture in the pan so it is flat and even.

4. Bake until light golden brown, 40 minutes. Remove the pan from the oven and allow the bars to cool for 20 minutes, but do not turn off the oven.

5. Using the parchment overhang, lift the bars out of the pan and place them on a cutting board. Using a chef's knife, cut in half lengthwise, then cut each half crosswise into 8 bars, for 16 bars total.

6. Coat a rimmed sheet pan with nonstick cooking spray and use a spatula to arrange the bars evenly on it, leaving a little space between each bar. Bake the bars again until they are golden brown, 15 to 20 minutes. This second baking crisps them up.

7. Transfer the sheet pan to a cooling rack. Let the bars cool completely before serving, about 1 hour. The granola bars can be stored in ziplock bags or other airtight containers for up to a week at room temperature.

tips & tweaks

● This recipe is highly tweakable! Use any nuts, like walnuts or pecans, instead of the almonds, and any dried fruit in place of the cranberries. Chopped apricots, dates, and dried cherries are great. Or skip the almond extract and use a teaspoon of vanilla instead, and change up the spices (try cardamom and allspice). If you don't like candied ginger, leave it out. As long as you keep the overall amounts of nuts, dried fruit, oats, egg whites, and oil the same, the specifics are negotiable. So, to sum up:

—— **best ingredients for granola** (pick one from each category) ——

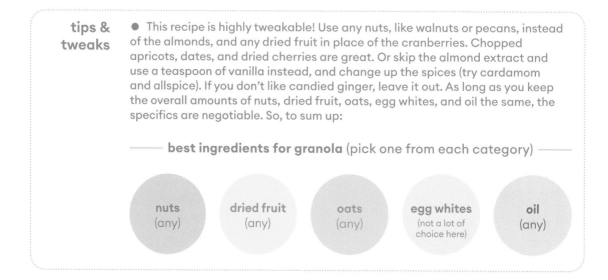

nuts (any) dried fruit (any) oats (any) egg whites (not a lot of choice here) oil (any)

Binge-Watch Popcorn
with a Punch

A heavy pot or Dutch oven heats popcorn more evenly than a regular pot, and you won't be picking out any burnt or unpopped kernels. The optional nutritional yeast, also called nooch (yes—*nooch!*), or one of the other variations, will punch this up and make it a dangerously addictive snack.

⅓ cup **oil** (sunflower, coconut, and grapeseed taste best, but olive oil and canola work, too)

½ cup **popcorn kernels**

½ teaspoon **fine sea salt**

the punch
(optional)

These seasonings can give your popcorn a flavor boost.

Umamicorn
2 to 3 tablespoons **nutritional yeast** and a large pinch of **cayenne pepper** or chile powder

Dessert Popcorn
2 tablespoons **brown sugar** and ½ teaspoon **ground cinnamon**

Pop Spice
½ to 1 teaspoon (add a little at a time, to taste) **ground cumin**, garam masala, or za'atar (See Rich Blends, below)

Buttercorn
2 to 4 tablespoons **unsalted butter** (go easy, because you're starting out with a lot of oil in the pot), melted

get it set

Put a large bowl for the popcorn next to the stove.

Set out all your ingredients.

1. In a large Dutch oven or other heavy-bottomed pot set over medium-high heat, combine the oil and 3 popcorn kernels and cover the pot. When you hear the kernels pop, remove the lid, add the remaining kernels, and partially cover the pot, leaving open a 1-inch crack to release the steam (face the crack away from you so the steam doesn't burn you). Reduce the heat to medium-low and cook until the popping stops, 2 to 5 minutes.

2. Using oven mitts, carefully pour the popcorn into the large bowl. Immediately toss it with the salt and one of the seasoning blends, if you like.

rich blends

Two great spice blends to keep on hand:

- **Garam masala** is an Indian spice blend that usually includes cumin, coriander, cinnamon, cardamom, clove, black pepper, and chile powder.

- **Za'atar** is a Middle Eastern herb and spice mix with thyme, sumac, and sesame.

Spicy, Crispy Kale Chips

SERVES 3 OR 4

Like potato chips—but kale! The trick to getting kale chips crispy is to make sure the kale is totally, thoroughly dry, and that you don't crowd the sheet pans. Otherwise the moisture from the kale will steam the leaves and make them soggy. These are great plain or spiced up with chili powder and other seasonings (see Tips & Tweaks).

1 large bunch **kale** (any kind is fine), stems removed and leaves torn into bite-size pieces (about 2 quarts), washed and dried (see How to Wash & Dry Salad Greens, page 150)

2 tablespoons **extra-virgin olive oil**

Kosher salt

Mild chili powder, for sprinkling (optional)

Nutritional yeast, for sprinkling (optional)

get it set

Heat the oven to 350°F.

Set out all your ingredients.

1. Make sure the kale is dry. If it feels even the littlest bit damp, spread out the leaves on one or two large, clean kitchen towels and pat them dry with another towel, turning the leaves over. Crinkly kale hides moisture in its ruffles, so look closely.

2. Put the kale into a large bowl, drizzle it with the olive oil, and sprinkle it lightly with salt. Toss the kale pieces well, massaging the oil onto each piece until the oil is evenly distributed and the kale is glistening.

3. Spread the kale out on two rimmed sheet pans, making sure the pieces don't overlap (if they do, you can work in batches, or use a third sheet pan). Bake the kale until the leaves look crispy and it crumbles if you nudge it with tongs, 12 to 16 minutes. Transfer the pans to wire racks and allow them to cool to room temperature.

4. Sprinkle the kale chips with the chili powder and nutritional yeast, if you like, and add a little more salt if needed.

> **tips & tweaks**
> - Don't use baby kale here. It is usually too delicate to stand up to the heat of the oven and may wilt rather than crisp up.
> - Add even more flavor by sprinkling the kale chips lightly before baking with any of the seasoning mixes used for the Crunchy Snack Crackeritos on page 58.

Noodles & Pasta

Not-Quite-Instant Ramen

SERVES 4

Traditional Japanese ramen is made with intense, long-simmered homemade stock and meticulously hand-pulled noodles. This may not be that, but it's richly flavored and deeply nourishing, with supple noodles and tender mushrooms seasoned to perfection with soy sauce and fish sauce. Serve it as is, or top it with a jammy egg or tofu, and you'll have an extremely tasty meal that's ready in under an hour.

Kosher salt, as needed

1 bunch **scallions**

3 ounces (about 1 packed cup) **shiitake mushroom caps** (optional)

1 (½-inch) piece **fresh ginger**, peeled (see How to Prep Ginger, page 86)

1 tablespoon **toasted (Asian) sesame oil**

1 **garlic clove**, thinly sliced (see Garlic Prep, page 13)

6 cups **chicken broth**, homemade (see page 184) or store-bought

1 (3-inch) square **kombu** (optional; see Kombu: Help from Kelp, page 78)

1 tablespoon **soy sauce** or **tamari**, or more to taste

1 tablespoon **Asian fish sauce**, or more to taste

12 ounces **dried ramen noodles**, or 24 ounces fresh ramen noodles

optional toppings

Ramen-style eggs (see Egg Academy, page 30)

Cubed **tofu**, any firmness you like

Shredded **cooked chicken**

Thinly sliced **cooked pork**

Sliced **scallion greens**

Sliced **dried seaweed snacks**

Sesame seeds

get it set

Put a colander in the sink.

Set out all your ingredients.

1. Fill a medium pot with water for the noodles. Stir in enough salt to make it taste like seawater (nicely salty, but not *too* salty). Place the pot on high heat and let the water come to a boil while you make the soup (it will take a while to boil).

2. Cut the green parts off the scallions and save them for an extra topping, if desired. Thinly slice the whites.

3. Slice the mushroom caps in half. The mushrooms are optional, but they do add a lot of flavor to the broth (and you can always fish them out afterward!).

4. Rest the flat side of a chef's knife on the ginger and smash it with the side of your fist. This helps release the essential oils.

5. Set a medium pot over medium-high heat and add the sesame oil. Let it heat up for about 20 seconds. It will thin out as it heats, but it shouldn't get hot enough to smoke. Stir in the scallion whites, mushrooms, garlic, and ginger, and cook until the scallions and mushrooms are tender, about 5 minutes.

(recipe continues)

6. Pour in the broth and 1 cup of water, and add the kombu if using. Bring to a simmer, then continue to simmer for 5 minutes. Season the broth to taste with soy sauce and fish sauce (they both add umami and salt). You're looking for a deep flavor that's on the verge of being salty, but not quite.

7. When the water for the noodles comes to a boil, add the ramen noodles and cook them according to the timing on the package, usually 1 to 5 minutes depending on whether they're fresh or dried (the fresh stuff cooks more quickly). To test it, grab a strand with a fork and run it under cold water before tasting (see Al Dente: The Tooth Test, page 95). Drain the noodles in the colander and run some cool water over them to get rid of some of the starch.

8. Divide the noodles equally among four bowls. Use a slotted spoon to add the mushrooms and scallions on top of the noodles, then pour in the broth. Add any additional toppings and serve immediately.

kombu: help from kelp

Kombu is a kind of dried kelp (a type of seaweed) that's often used in Japanese cooking to add umami and salty richness (as well as some nutrients and minerals) to soups, stews, and other dishes. Because it's dried, it will last for months, so it's always worth grabbing some whenever you find it. To use it, cut the kelp into whatever size piece your recipe calls for (usually a 3- or 4-inch square) and drop it in the pot. Any whitish powder covering the kombu is just the minerals, and that's where the flavor is. You don't need to wipe it off!

tips & tweaks

● To make vegan ramen, use vegetable broth instead of chicken broth, and skip the fish sauce, adding more soy sauce; or use coconut amino acids if you have them.

● Ramen is often made with a rich pork broth, which some butcher shops and Asian markets sell. You can substitute it here for the chicken broth.

Fast Pho

Pho (pronounced "fuh") is a rich Vietnamese noodle soup loaded with tender bits of beef or chicken and tons of fresh herbs and bean sprouts, and is traditionally simmered for hours or even days. This recipe is much faster, using store-bought beef broth zapped with ginger, garlic, star anise, and cinnamon, that gets close to the amazing complexity of the slow-cooked original.

1 pound **eye of round** or other lean steak, fat trimmed, frozen (see Tips & Tweaks, page 80)

6 cups **beef stock**

1 (3-inch) piece **fresh ginger,** peeled and cut into 4 slices (see How to Prep Ginger, page 86)

3 **garlic cloves,** smashed and peeled (see Garlic Prep, page 13)

3 **whole star anise pods**

1 (1-inch-long) piece **cinnamon stick**

½ **fresh green chile,** such as jalapeño (optional)

2 teaspoons **light brown sugar,** or more to taste

2 teaspoons **Asian fish sauce,** or more to taste

8 ounces **rice noodles** (see Tips & Tweaks, page 80)

for serving

Thinly sliced **onion** (see Onion Prep, page 12)

Bean sprouts

Cilantro leaves and tender sprigs

Thai basil or regular basil leaves and tender sprigs

Lime or **lemon wedges**

get it set

Remove the frozen beef from the freezer and let it sit at room temperature for 15 minutes to thaw slightly.

Set out all your other ingredients.

1. Using a chef's knife, slice the meat as thin as you can; the thinner the better here. If the meat is too frozen to slice, let it sit for 5 to 10 minutes longer. Then let the slices sit at room temperature until needed.

2. In a large pot, combine the stock, ginger, garlic, star anise, cinnamon stick, and chile if using. Cover, bring to a simmer, and continue to simmer for 15 to 30 minutes. Taste the broth: When it is rich and gingery, it's ready. Use a slotted spoon to remove the ginger, garlic, star anise, cinnamon stick, and chile.

3. Stir in the brown sugar and the fish sauce, taste, and then add more sugar if it needs more sweetness, or more fish sauce if it tastes flat (fish sauce adds salt plus umami flavors).

(recipe continues)

4. While the broth is still simmering, fill a medium pot with water and bring it to a boil. Turn off the heat and add noodles, then stir to make sure the noodles don't stick together. Let the noodles sit in the hot water until they have softened, 5 to 10 minutes, then drain them in a colander.

5. To serve, reheat the broth to a simmer. If you prefer your beef well-done, add the beef slices to the simmering broth and let them cook until they are done to your taste, 1 to 3 minutes. Heap the noodles in four large bowls. Divide the beef slices (either cooked or raw) and the onions among the bowls, and ladle in the hot broth. (The hot broth will cook the raw beef, leaving it rare and juicy.) Top each bowl with the sprouts, cilantro, and basil, and serve the pho with lime wedges on the side for squeezing into the soup.

tips & tweaks

● It's much easier to slice beef into super-thin pieces when it's frozen. If your beef isn't already frozen, place it in the freezer for at least 1 hour before slicing. Or else you can buy very thinly sliced beef at an Asian supermarket.

● Any shape of rice noodle will work here. Typically, pho recipes call for rice stick noodles, which are flat in shape. But some recipes use rice thread, or vermicelli, noodles instead, which are much thinner and tubular. Any noodle made of rice flour and water will work here; even thick rice noodles have a neutral taste that won't overpower the complex flavor of the beef broth.

● To make **Chicken Pho,** substitute chicken stock for the beef stock, and add sliced skinless raw chicken (breast or thigh meat) to the pot after the broth has come to a simmer in Step 5. Let the chicken cook in the broth until done (if you cut a piece, it won't be pink on the inside—see Chicken: Is It Done Yet?, page 110). Continue with the recipe as directed.

Pan-Fried Ginger Noodles

This beauty is garlicky, gingery, and as spicy as you dare—it's best when it bites back just a little. Most of the prep time for this East Asian–influenced pan-fried noodle dish is spent slicing (have your chef's knife ready). Once that's done, the dish comes together in minutes.

1 cup thinly sliced **scallions** (about 1 bunch, both white and green parts)

3 tablespoons **soy sauce** or **tamari**, or more to taste

1 tablespoon **grated fresh ginger** (see How to Prep Ginger, page 86)

2 teaspoons **rice vinegar** or **sherry vinegar**

1 teaspoon **toasted (Asian) sesame oil**

¼ teaspoon **kosher salt**

6 ounces **soba noodles, rice noodles,** or **thin spaghetti**

2 tablespoons **peanut** or **grapeseed oil,** plus more for tossing

5 **garlic cloves,** thinly sliced (see Garlic Prep, page 13)

½ cup / 65 grams thawed frozen **peas** or shelled edamame (optional)

1 to 2 teaspoons **Sriracha,** sambal oelek, or other hot sauce, or to taste

Juice of ½ **lime,** or to taste

1 cup **fresh cilantro leaves**

2 tablespoons **sesame seeds** or chopped **roasted peanuts** (optional)

get it set

Put a colander in the sink.

Place a plate or sheet pan next to the sink.

Set out all your ingredients.

1. Fill a pot with water for the noodles. Place it on high heat and let the water come to a boil while you start making the sauce (it will take a while to boil).

2. In a small bowl, combine the scallions, soy sauce, ginger, vinegar, sesame oil, and salt. Set aside.

3. When the water comes to a boil, add the noodles and cook for only half the time listed on the package directions (the noodles should still be quite firm but not breakable). Carefully drain the noodles in the colander and then, while they are still in the colander, toss them with a little oil. Spread the noodles out on the plate or sheet pan to keep them from sticking together.

(recipe continues)

4. In a large skillet over medium heat, heat 2 tablespoons peanut oil for about 20 seconds. It will thin out as it heats, but it shouldn't get hot enough to smoke. Add the garlic and cook until it is crisp and pale golden around the edges, 1 to 2 minutes. Keep an eye on it–garlic burns really quickly. If the garlic starts to turn brown, pull the pan off the heat to let it cool down for a few seconds. Add half of the scallion mixture (save the other half for later) and use a wooden spoon or tongs to fry and toss the mixture until it is fragrant, about 1 minute.

5. Raise the heat to high and add the noodles. Fry, tossing and mixing, until the noodles are hot and lightly coated with the sauce, about 30 seconds. Add the peas if using, the Sriracha, and the remaining scallion mixture. Continue to stir-fry until the peas heat up, 1 to 2 minutes. Remove the pan from the heat and stir in the lime juice. Serve garnished with the cilantro and sesame seeds.

tips & tweaks

- Because the sauce for this recipe is so intensely salty and pungent, you don't need to salt the noodle cooking water.

- The key to this dish is to boil the noodles until they are only halfway done (they should be pliable but still firm in the center). They will finish cooking when you panfry them.

- You can swap the peas or edamame for 2 cups of (choose one):
  - Baby spinach or other greens
  - Sliced radishes
  - Corn kernels

- To make it meaty or mushroomy, add either of these to the pan after the garlic browns:
  - ½ **pound ground meat** (pork, turkey, and chicken work well) or vegan meat
  - **1 cup sliced shiitake caps.**

Let the meat or mushrooms cook until golden (about 5 minutes) before adding the scallion mixture.

Chill Peanut Sesame Noodles

This dish, inspired by my favorite Chinese American takeout, is so easygoing it works anywhere you take it—the lunchroom, the dinner table, or even right out of the fridge as a snack. Noodles get along with almost any vegetable, so you can improvise a topping from whatever's around. These noodles are as flexible as they come.

for the veggies

- 2 **celery stalks** or **carrots**
- 1 cup sliced **cucumber** (peeled if you like) or shredded romaine lettuce
- 2 teaspoons **toasted (Asian) sesame oil**
- 1½ teaspoons **rice vinegar**
- ¼ teaspoon **kosher salt**

for the noodles

- **Kosher salt**, as needed
- 1 pound **thin spaghetti** or **rice noodles**
- ¼ cup **soy sauce** or **tamari**
- 3 tablespoons **toasted (Asian) sesame oil**
- 3 tablespoons **rice vinegar**
- 3 tablespoons **tahini**
- 3 tablespoons smooth **peanut butter**, preferably natural, without added sugar
- 1½ tablespoons **dark brown sugar**
- 1 fat **garlic clove**, peeled (see Garlic Prep, page 13)
- 1 (1-inch) piece **fresh ginger**, peeled (see How to Prep Ginger, page 86)

- ½ cup chopped **toasted peanuts** (either salted or unsalted), for serving (optional)
- Chopped **fresh cilantro, celery leaves**, or other soft herbs, for serving

get it set

Put a colander in the sink.

Set out all your ingredients.

1. Fill a pot with water for the noodles, then stir in enough salt to make it taste like seawater (nicely salty, but not *too* salty). Place the pot on high heat and let the water come to a boil while you make the topping.

2. Make the vegetable topping: Put the celery and cucumber in a medium bowl. Add the sesame oil, vinegar, and salt and toss. Set it aside for later. (If you are using shredded lettuce, wait to add it just before serving.)

3. Cook the noodles and make the sauce: Add the noodles to the boiling water and cook according to the timing on the package (or a minute less—taste a strand to see when it's ready; see Al Dente: The Tooth Test, page 95). Drain in the colander in the sink, then give the noodles a quick rinse with cold water from the tap.

(recipe continues)

4. While the noodles are cooking, in a large bowl that will hold the noodles when they're done cooking, whisk together the soy sauce, sesame oil, rice vinegar, tahini, peanut butter, and brown sugar. Taste, and add a little salt if it needs it (if your peanut butter is unsalted, it might).

5. Use a Microplane or other fine grater to grate the garlic into the sauce in the bowl. Grate in the ginger (you don't need to wash the grater; it's fine if it's still a little garlicky). Stir everything together.

6. When the noodles are done draining, give the colander a shake to get rid of any excess water, and add them to the dressing in the bowl. Use tongs to gently toss the noodles in the peanut mixture. To serve, top the noodles with the chopped peanuts, if using, the vegetable topping, the lettuce if using, and the cilantro or other herbs.

how to prep ginger

The best tool for peeling ginger is actually a teaspoon, rather than a vegetable peeler or a paring knife.

Using the edge of the spoon, scrape away the papery skin until you see the yellow flesh underneath. If the small knobs on the surface are hard to peel, use the spoon's edge to cut them off.

To grate ginger, use a Microplane or any fine grater. Grate the peeled ginger with a fair amount of pressure. Don't forget to scrape the ginger pulp off the back of the grater, where most of it will try to hide.

tips & tweaks

● The peanut sauce is also great on a grain bowl (see pages 136 to 142) or to use as dip for veggies or rice crackers—or both.

● Substitute cashew or almond butter for the peanut butter if peanuts aren't your thing.

Crunchy-Top Mac and Cheese

Mac and cheese is already so silky, creamy, and comforting that it's hard to top—except maybe with a great topping. This light, crunchy bread-crumb-and-Parmesan crust adds a delicious crispness on top of the classic dish. The high heat allows the macaroni to cook in its own ultrarich, creamy sauce. So what do you say? Easier? Check. Tastier?? Check! My friends, I think we're done here.

4½ cups **whole milk**

8 ounces (1 brick) **cream cheese**, at room temperature

1½ teaspoons **kosher salt**

1 teaspoon **dry mustard powder**

½ teaspoon **freshly ground black pepper**

¼ teaspoon **cayenne pepper** (optional)

¼ teaspoon freshly grated **nutmeg**

1½ cups / 90 grams **panko bread crumbs** (see Tips & Tweaks)

⅔ cup / 65 grams **grated Parmesan cheese**

4 tablespoons / ½ stick / 57 grams **unsalted butter**, melted, plus more for the baking dish

1 pound **macaroni pasta**

5 cups / 1 pound grated **sharp** or **extra-sharp cheddar cheese**

get it set

Take the cream cheese out of the fridge 30 to 60 minutes ahead to allow it to soften.

Heat the oven to 425°F.

Butter a 9 x 13-inch baking dish.

Set out all your other ingredients.

1. In a blender or food processor, blend the milk, cream cheese, salt, mustard powder, black pepper, cayenne, if using, and nutmeg until smooth. This may take 2 to 3 minutes if you're starting with cold cream cheese.

2. In a medium bowl, mix together the bread crumbs, Parmesan, and melted butter until the crumbs are coated with butter.

3. Put the macaroni and the cheddar into the baking dish and mix them together really well so the cheese is well dispersed amid the pasta. Pour in the milk mixture and carefully give everything a good stir. Sprinkle the bread-crumb mixture evenly on top.

4. Bake for 20 minutes, then raise the heat to 450°F and continue to bake until the top is golden and bubbling, 15 to 25 minutes longer. Remove the pan from the oven and let it sit for at least 10 minutes before serving. Serve hot or warm.

● Panko is a Japanese style of bread crumb made from light, crustless bread. Because it's so airy, it absorbs less oil and stays crispier and fluffier than regular dense bread crumbs when baked or fried.

● If you want to work ahead a little (up to 8 hours before you want to eat), put the macaroni, cheese, and milk mixture in the baking dish; mix up the bread-crumb mixture but keep it separate; and store everything in the fridge. Right before you want to bake it, sprinkle the topping on the mac and cheese and bake as directed in Step 4.

● I love to swap in a mix of cheddar and Gruyère (or Jarlsberg) instead of using all cheddar. In fact you can use any firm cheese you've got.

Home-Base Spaghetti

Is there anyone who doesn't love twirling tomato-coated spaghetti on a fork? This dish is basic in the best sense, and it's worth mastering for any pasta-loving cook. It's comforting served by itself or topped with meatballs to make the straight-up classic (see Tips & Tweaks). Make extra sauce! This tomato sauce can be used any time a marinara sauce is called for, and the leftovers freeze perfectly (see Tips & Tweaks).

1 (28-ounce) can **whole plum tomatoes**

2 tablespoons **extra-virgin olive oil**, plus more for drizzling

2 **garlic cloves**, thinly sliced (see Garlic Prep, page 13)

Pinch of **crushed red pepper flakes** (optional)

¼ teaspoon **freshly ground black pepper**

2 sprigs **fresh basil**, plus more, thinly sliced leaves for serving

Kosher salt, as needed

1 pound **spaghetti** (or other pasta shape)

Grated Parmesan cheese (optional)

get it set

Put a colander in the sink.

Set out all your ingredients.

1. Place the tomatoes with their juices in a medium bowl. Break them up into large chunky pieces with kitchen scissors, a wooden spoon, or your fingers.

2. Place a large skillet over medium-high heat, add the oil, and let it heat up for about 20 seconds. It will thin out as it heats, but it shouldn't get hot enough to smoke. Stir in the garlic, the red paper flakes if using, and the black pepper, and cook for 1 to 2 minutes, until the garlic starts to turn light gold in spots. Keep an eye on it: If the garlic starts to turn brown, pull the pan off the heat to let it cool down for a few seconds.

3. Stir in the tomatoes, basil sprigs, and ½ teaspoon salt and bring the mixture to a simmer. Turn the heat to medium-low and cook, stirring occasionally, for about 25 minutes, until the tomatoes break down and the mixture looks like a chunky tomato sauce. Keep adjusting the heat if you need to. The sauce should cook at a brisk simmer, not at a boil.

4. Fill a pot with water for the pasta, then stir in enough salt to make it taste like seawater (nicely salty, but not *too* salty). Place the pot on high heat and let the water come to a boil while the sauce simmers.

5. When the water comes to a boil, add the pasta and cook it until it is al dente, about a minute less than the timing on the package. To test it, grab a strand with a fork and run it under cold water before tasting (see Al Dente: The Tooth Test, page 95).

6. When the pasta is done to taste, drain it in the colander in the sink, then return it to the empty pasta pot.

7. Pluck the basil sprigs out of the sauce and discard them. Taste the sauce and add more salt if needed. Add some of the sauce to the pasta in the pot. Toss gently until the pasta is coated with sauce (you may not need all of it, depending on how saucy you like it). Add Parmesan, if using, and gently toss again. Serve it immediately, topped with sliced basil and a drizzle of olive oil.

---

tips & tweaks

● The sauce recipe on its own makes 3 cups, enough for 6 to 10 helpings of spaghetti. It freezes well for up to 6 months.

● For classic spaghetti and meatballs, cook the meatballs on page 123 beforehand, and add them to the sauce for the last 5 minutes of simmering.

● To make a very **Simple Tomato Meat Sauce**, add 1 pound ground meat (beef, turkey, or any other meat, or vegan meat) to the pan along with the garlic in Step 2. Sear the meat, stirring it, until it browns in spots and is no longer pink, about 8 minutes. Then proceed with Step 3.

Pesto Pasta
with Mozz Topping

Pesto and pasta are already a perfect couple, and here the rich texture of fresh mozzarella on top of that might qualify this dish as Greatest of All Time. The heat of the pesto pasta melts the cheese just a little, but not all the way, leaving it soft and velvety.

Kosher salt, as needed

⅓ cup **pine nuts** or **slivered almonds**

2 **garlic cloves,** peeled (see Garlic Prep, page 13)

5 cups packed **fresh basil leaves** (from about 5 ounces basil sprigs or 2 medium bunches)

¾ cup **extra-virgin olive oil,** plus more for serving

⅓ cup / 35 grams **grated Parmesan cheese,** plus more for serving

1 pound **pasta** (spiral shapes, such as rotini or fusilli, work really well here to catch the pesto in their crevices)

8 ounces **fresh mozzarella,** torn into bite-size chunks

Freshly ground black pepper

get it set

Put a colander in the sink.

Set out all your ingredients.

1. Fill a pot with water for the pasta, then stir in enough salt to make it taste like seawater (nicely salty, but not *too* salty). Place the pot on high heat and let the water come to a boil while you start making the pesto (it will take a while to boil).

2. Meanwhile, put a small skillet over medium heat and add the nuts. Let them toast, stirring once or twice, until they are golden and fragrant, about 3 minutes. Immediately pour the nuts into a food processor or blender, and add the garlic cloves. Pulse a few times to chop everything up. Add the basil and ½ teaspoon salt, and pulse until the basil is mostly chopped. You'll probably have to stop the machine and scrape down the sides of the bowl with a rubber spatula to get everything evenly chopped.

3. With the food processor or blender running, slowly drizzle in the oil until everything's combined and smooth. Add the Parmesan and process briefly to combine. Taste, and stir in more salt if necessary.

(recipe continues)

4. When the water comes to a boil, add the pasta and cook it until it is al dente, about a minute less than the timing on the package. To test it, grab a piece with a fork and run it under cold water before tasting (see Al Dente: The Tooth Test, opposite).

5. Using a measuring cup or a mug, scoop out about a cup of the pasta water and put it aside to use later. Carefully drain the pasta in the colander, then return it to the pot.

6. Add the pesto to the pasta and toss gently to combine, adding a splash of the reserved pasta cooking water if it looks dry. Fold in the mozzarella, taking care not to smush it. Serve immediately, topping each serving with some Parmesan, a drizzle of oil, and some freshly ground black pepper.

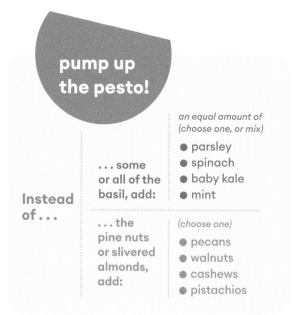

pump up the pesto!

Instead of . . .

. . . some or all of the basil, add:

an equal amount of (choose one, or mix)
- parsley
- spinach
- baby kale
- mint

. . . the pine nuts or slivered almonds, add:

(choose one)
- pecans
- walnuts
- cashews
- pistachios

tips & tweaks

● Some cooks swear that pesto tastes better when made in a mortar and pestle rather than a food processor. If you want to try it out, let's go: Put the basil, ½ teaspoon salt, the garlic cloves, and nuts in a mortar and pound it with a pestle until you get a uniform green paste. Then drip in the oil, a little at a time, grinding as you go. (Don't try to add the oil until the garlic-basil-nut mixture is finely mashed and smooth. If you do, it will slosh around and you won't be able to pound down the particles. From that point it will be more about mixing than grinding, and you won't get the texture you want.)

● To increase the veggie factor, take a handful of halved cherry tomatoes or thawed frozen peas, or a few cups of baby spinach, and fold them in with the mozzarella.

● Add other herbs or greens to pesto, or switch up the nuts to change the flavor. Mix and match: mint + basil + pistachio is especially tasty. For other possible pesto paths, see above.

Al Dente
The Tooth Test

Al dente (al-DEN-tay) is Italian for "to the tooth," meaning the pasta (or rice) is still firm when you bite it, not mushy. It's the point where pasta tastes and feels best–chewy, not hard, but tender.

The only way to check for al dente pasta is to taste it. Start sampling your pasta a minute or two before the package instructions say it should be done. Use a slotted spoon or a fork to remove a piece of pasta from the pot, and rinse it under cold water so it doesn't burn your mouth. When you bite into it, you should feel some resistance to your teeth, but not a hard crunch. When you do, strain the pasta quickly, because it will keep cooking for a minute or so after you take it out of the water.

You can even see that slight resistance in the middle of the pasta: there may be a thin white ring in the center of the strand of pasta where you bit it. Think of this as the spine of the pasta. Spineless pasta is just a big wet noodle!

Fresh-made pasta cooks faster than dried pasta, and perfectly cooked fresh pasta feels a little softer in your mouth than dried. Generally, fresh pasta cooks somewhere between 1 and 3 minutes, depending on the noodle's thickness, and it will float to the top of the pot when it's al dente. Cooked fresh pasta should still have some bite to it, but less than dried pasta. Check fresh pasta often as it cooks–it can go from perfectly al dente to overcooked and mushy in seconds.

Summer Pasta
with Ricotta & Cherry Tomatoes

Juicy, fresh tomatoes team up with creamy, rich ricotta to make an easy, bright pasta topping. Cherry tomatoes are sweetest in the summer, but even in the winter, when the tomatoes are a little tangier, this is pretty great. It always tastes like summer vacation to me, whenever I eat it. The large amount of mint or basil adds freshness, but you can leave it off, no biggie.

Kosher salt, as needed

6 tablespoons **extra-virgin olive oil**

5 **garlic cloves**, thinly sliced (see Garlic Prep, page 13)

2 pints **cherry tomatoes**, preferably in many colors, cut in half, divided

1 pound **short pasta shapes**, such as fusilli or farfalle (bow ties)

2 tablespoons / 28 grams **unsalted butter**

1¾ to 2 cups (15 to 16 ounces) **fresh whole-milk ricotta** (see Tips & Tweaks)

Freshly ground black pepper, as needed

½ cup / 6 grams **fresh mint** or **basil leaves** (optional)

get it set

Put a colander in the sink.

Set out all your ingredients.

1. Fill a pot with water for the pasta, then stir in enough salt to make it taste like seawater (nicely salty, but not *too* salty). Place the pot on high heat and let the water come to a boil while you start making the sauce (it will take a while to boil).

2. In a large skillet over medium-high heat, heat the oil for about 20 seconds. It will thin out as it heats, but it shouldn't get hot enough to smoke. Stir in the garlic and cook for about 1 minute, or until you can smell it. Keep an eye on it–garlic burns really quickly. If the garlic starts to turn brown, pull the pan off the heat to let it cool down for a few seconds. Add about two-thirds of the cherry tomatoes to the pan, reserving the rest. Cook until the tomatoes just start to shrivel up and release their juices, 2 to 4 minutes.

3. Stir in the remaining cherry tomatoes and 1 teaspoon salt, and turn off the heat. Let the pan sit while the pasta cooks.

4. When the water comes to a boil, add the pasta and cook it until it is al dente, about a minute less than the timing on the package. To test it, grab a piece with a fork and run it under cold water before tasting (see Al Dente: The Tooth Test, page 95).

5. Using a measuring cup or a mug, scoop out about a cup of pasta water and put it aside to use later. Carefully drain the pasta in the colander, then return it to the dry pot.

6. Turn the heat back on under the tomatoes. Add ¼ cup of the reserved pasta water and the butter, and bring to a simmer to let the sauce come together. It will start out watery, but the starch from the pasta water will thicken it in 2 or 3 minutes.

7. Add the tomato mixture to the cooked pasta, stirring gently to coat the pasta. If it looks too dry, add a splash more pasta water.

8. Transfer the pasta to serving plates, and dollop with half of the ricotta. Top with black pepper, sprinkle with mint leaves if using, and serve immediately, with the rest of the ricotta on the side for people to add on their own.

---

tips & tweaks

● Most ricotta is sold in containers that weigh 15 to 16 ounces (1¾ to 2 cups). Use either one, because ¼ cup more or less ricotta just doesn't matter here. If you can't get fresh ricotta, or aren't a ricotta fan, substitute about 8 ounces cubed fresh mozzarella. The pasta will be less creamy and more gooey, and there's nothing wrong with gooey.

Garlicky, Crumb-y Pasta

SERVES 4

This pasta is my daughter Dahlia's all-time favorite, and we make it together two or three times a month. Its beauty is in the crunchy, garlicky topping on the springy, buttery noodles—so we keep this pretty plain, though sometimes I'll add sliced olives or an egg (see Tips & Tweaks). Anchovies add a subtle, savory flavor that's delicious and not at all fishy.

Kosher salt, as needed

¼ cup **extra-virgin olive oil**

6 **garlic cloves**, minced (see Garlic Prep, page 13)

4 to 8 **oil-packed anchovy fillets**, chopped

Pinch of **crushed red pepper flakes** (optional)

1 cup / 60 grams **panko** or other **unseasoned bread crumbs**

1 pound **spaghetti, linguine**, or other pasta

4 tablespoons / ½ stick / 57 grams **unsalted butter**

½ cup / 6 grams chopped **fresh parsley leaves**

Lemon wedges, for serving

Flaky sea salt, for serving

Freshly ground black pepper, for serving

get it set

Put a colander in the sink.

Put a plate next to the stove for the bread crumbs.

Set out all your ingredients.

1. Fill a pot with water for the pasta, then stir in enough kosher salt to make it taste like seawater (nicely salty, but not *too* salty). Place the pot on high heat and let the water come to a boil while you start to make the topping (it will take a while to boil).

2. Meanwhile, in a large skillet set over medium-high heat, heat the oil for about 20 seconds. It will thin out as it heats, but it shouldn't get hot enough to smoke. Stir in the garlic, anchovies, and red pepper flakes if using. Cook until fragrant, about 1 minute. Keep an eye on it—garlic burns really quickly. If the garlic starts to turn brown, pull the pan off the heat to let it cool down for a few seconds. The anchovies will have mostly dissolved in the oil.

3. Stir in the bread crumbs and continue to cook, stirring frequently, until the bread crumbs are golden brown, 3 to 4 minutes. Using a large spoon, transfer the bread crumbs to the plate.

(recipe continues)

4. When the water is boiling, add the pasta and cook until it is just shy of al dente, about 2 minutes less than the package directions. To test it, grab a piece with a fork and run it under cool water before tasting (see Al Dente: The Tooth Test, page 95). Using a measuring cup or a mug, scoop out about a cup of the pasta water and put it aside to use in the next step. Carefully drain the pasta in the colander.

5. In the same pot you cooked the pasta in, melt the butter over medium-high heat. Whisk in ¾ cup of the reserved pasta water and bring it to a simmer. Simmer for 1 minute to reduce the sauce, then turn off the heat. Add the pasta and the parsley, and toss to coat. Let simmer for another 30 seconds to 1 minute to heat through and finish cooking the pasta. Add a splash more pasta water if the pasta seems dry.

6. Right before serving, toss about three-quarters of the bread crumbs with the pasta until well distributed. Divide the pasta among four bowls, and top with the remaining bread crumbs, a squeeze of lemon juice, a sprinkle of flaky sea salt, and lots of black pepper.

tips & tweaks

● If you want to work ahead, the bread crumbs will keep in the fridge for up to 1 week. Put them back in a skillet and warm them over low heat until they get crispy again. They're ready when you can smell the garlic.

● Sliced olives make this even saltier. Add 2 tablespoons to the pan along with the parsley.

● If you must leave out the anchovies, okay fine. Just before serving, sprinkle the pasta with lots of grated Parmesan cheese or a little extra salt.

● Top each serving of the pasta with a poached or fried egg (see Egg Academy, page 30). The silky, runny yolk is fantastic with the crunchy bread crumbs.

The Baked Ziti Zone

Big tomatoey pans of baked pasta? Caps of melty cheese singed brown in the oven? You're in the Ziti Zone, and it's about as cozy and comforting as pasta gets. This one plays it straight, because classic baked ziti is hard to improve on. If you want to go rogue, though, add sausage or bacon (see Tips & Tweaks) for a meaty appeal. You'll still be in the zone.

Kosher salt, as needed

2 tablespoons **extra-virgin olive oil**

1 large **onion**, diced (see Onion Prep, page 12)

4 fat **garlic cloves**, minced (see Garlic Prep, page 13)

1½ teaspoons **dried oregano** or **Italian seasoning**

½ teaspoon **freshly ground black pepper**

6 cups **tomato sauce**, either store-bought or homemade (make a double batch of the sauce from Home-Base Spaghetti, page 90)

1 pound **ziti pasta** (or rigatoni, or penne)

15 to 16 ounces **whole-milk ricotta cheese** (see Tips & Tweaks)

2 cups / 8 ounces shredded **mozzarella**

⅔ cup / 70 grams **grated Parmesan cheese**

½ cup / 20 grams chopped **fresh basil** or **parsley** (optional)

get it set

Heat the oven to 400°F.

Put a colander in the sink.

Set out all your ingredients.

1. Fill a pot with water for the pasta, then stir in enough salt to make it taste like seawater (nicely salty, but not *too* salty). Place the pot on high heat and let the water come to a boil while you start making the sauce (it will take a while to boil).

2. Meanwhile, in a large pot, heat the oil over medium-high heat. Stir in the onion and cook, stirring occasionally, until light golden and starting to brown, about 8 minutes. Stir in the garlic, oregano, and black pepper, and cook for 1 minute. Keep an eye on it– garlic burns really quickly.

3. Stir in the tomato sauce and bring to a simmer. Reduce the heat to maintain the simmer, and cook, stirring occasionally, for 10 minutes to blend the flavors. Taste, and add more salt if it needs it.

4. When the water is boiling, cook the ziti until 3 minutes shy of al dente; check the timing on the box and subtract 3 minutes from the lower end of the cooking range (the ziti will finish cooking as you bake it).

(recipe continues)

Drain the pasta in the colander and quickly run some cold water over it to stop it from cooking in the residual heat. Give the colander a shake to get rid of the excess water, and return the pasta to the pot.

5. Stir half of the tomato sauce into the cooked pasta. Dollop with the ricotta and give the pasta a couple of stirs, just until the ricotta starts to blend in (mostly blended, but with a few white streaks of ricotta still distinct).

6. Spread ½ cup of the remaining tomato sauce on the bottom of a 9 x 13-inch baking dish. Scoop half the pasta mixture on top and spread it out in an even layer.

7. Sprinkle half of the mozzarella and half of the Parmesan over the pasta.

8. Scoop the rest of the pasta mixture on top of the cheeses, and spread it out in an even layer. Scrape the rest of the sauce over the pasta, spreading it to the edges. Sprinkle the rest of the mozzarella and Parmesan on top.

9. Bake until bubbly and golden, about 25 minutes. If you'd like a little more browning on the cheese, pop the baking dish under the broiler for 1 to 2 minutes.

10. Let the baked ziti cool for 10 minutes. Then scatter the basil on top, if you like, and serve.

tips & tweaks

- Most ricotta is sold in containers that weigh 15 to 16 ounces (1¾ to 2 cups). Use either one, because ¼ cup more or less ricotta just doesn't matter here.

- Any tubular pasta shape works; you want something hollow that can catch the sauce.

- Spreading the final layer of sauce all the way to the edges helps keep the pasta underneath from drying out.

- You can prepare and assemble this dish ahead of time, through Step 8. Keep it covered in the fridge for up to 2 days. Then bake it straight from the fridge, adding 5 to 10 minutes to the baking time to get it golden on top.

- Put some zip in your sauce! After the sauce is cooked, stir in a cup or two of chopped cooked veggies (broccoli, cauliflower, spinach, or mushrooms) or sliced cooked sausage. Or chop 2 or 3 strips of bacon and sauté them along with the onions in Step 2 before adding the garlic.

Sheet Pan
Fever

Epic Whole Roast Chicken

SERVES 4

Once you serve a whole roast chicken, you're a hero. Roast chicken dazzles when it has a tender, crispy, golden outside and a juicy, moist inside, so think of the sheet pan as your secret weapon: It makes the skin extra crispy and brown because the pan's low sides allow more heat circulation, and this helps the skin brown evenly without overcooking the meat. A roasting pan or ovenproof skillet will work almost as well, so use what you've got. If you add the optional veggies (see Tips & Tweaks), you'll have a whole meal and only one secret weapon to clean.

1 **whole chicken** (3½ to 4 pounds)

2 teaspoons **kosher salt**

1 teaspoon **freshly ground black pepper**

Small bunch of **mixed fresh herbs,** such as rosemary, thyme, and/or sage (optional)

Lemon wedges, for serving (optional)

get it set

Heat the oven to 450°F (unless you're putting the seasoned chicken in the fridge overnight).

Set out all your ingredients.

1. Pat the chicken dry with paper towels. This will help crisp up the skin (damp skin creates steam that could make it rubbery and prevent browning).

2. In a small bowl, mix together the salt and pepper. Using your hands, rub the mixture all over the chicken, inside the cavity and all over the outside. If you have time, put the chicken, uncovered, in the fridge for 1 hour or even overnight. Leaving it uncovered makes sure the skin stays dry for the all-important oven-crisping. Wash your hands well after handling the raw chicken.

3. When you're ready to roast the chicken, heat the oven to 450°F if you haven't done so yet.

4. Place the chicken, breast-side up, on a rimmed sheet pan (or in a roasting pan or an ovenproof skillet). Stuff the cavity of the chicken with the herbs, if you're using them.

5. Roast the chicken for 50 to 60 minutes. You don't have to turn it over or baste it or anything. It's done when the skin is golden brown and crisp, and when the chicken's juices run clear when a thigh is pierced with a knife (see Chicken: Is It Done Yet?, page 110).

6. Using oven mitts, remove the pan from the oven and let the chicken rest for 10 minutes before transferring it to a cutting board to carve. This allows the chicken to re-absorb some of its juices.

7. Carve (see How to Carve a Chicken, page 108) and serve the chicken with some of the pan juices and with lemon wedges for squeezing, if using.

tips & tweaks

● Make it a whole dinner by adding vegetables to the pan with the chicken. Cut into ½-inch chunks, these will cook in the same amount of time as the chicken:

- **Carrots**
- **Celery**
- **Brussels sprouts**
- **Mushrooms**
- **Sweet potatoes**
- **Onions** (sliced ¼ inch thick; see Onion Prep, page 12)

Surround the chicken with any one or a combination of these vegetables in one layer, leaving a little space between them and the bird so the steam escaping from the vegetables won't get in the way of the chicken skin crisping. That way your veggies should caramelize and crisp up, too.

● If you'd like to tie the chicken's legs together for a neater presentation, as pictured here, use a piece of kitchen string to tie them together, then cut them free after roasting.

How to Carve a Chicken

Although you *could* pull apart your gorgeous roast chicken with your bare hands, it's a lot easier and more presentable to use a knife. Let's walk through it.

1. Place the roast chicken on a cutting board, breast-side up.

2. Remove the leg (drumstick and thigh): Gently pull one of the legs away from the rest of the bird. Slice through the skin between the thigh and the body, then down through the joint at the base of the thigh. You may have to wiggle the knife blade a little to find the joint, but it will cut easily when you do. Remove the other leg the same way.

3. Separate the drumstick from the thigh: Place the leg on the cutting board and cut through the joint at the top of the drumstick. (The joint becomes more visible if you tug the parts gently away from each other.) Separate the other leg the same way.

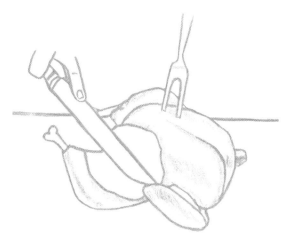

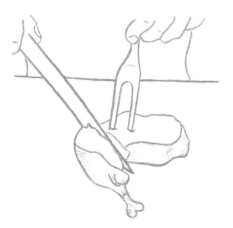

4. **Remove the breast meat:** Make a deep vertical cut, from front to back, along one side of the breastbone. Using the breastbone as a guide, slip the knife underneath the meat and remove the entire half breast with the wing still attached. Set it aside and repeat on the other breast half. You can leave the chicken breasts in one piece, or you can slice them, but either way make sure to include the crispy skin.

5. **Separate the wing from the breast:** Cut through the shoulder joint between the wing and the breast. Repeat with the other wing.

6. The tail just needs a little cut to get it off. My favorite part, it's all skin and fat. Yum.

7. To separate the meat from the bones to use for a salad or other dish, wait until the chicken has cooled and then use your fingers to pull the meat from the bones. Save the carcass, including the bones, to make a rich and hearty chicken stock (see page 184).

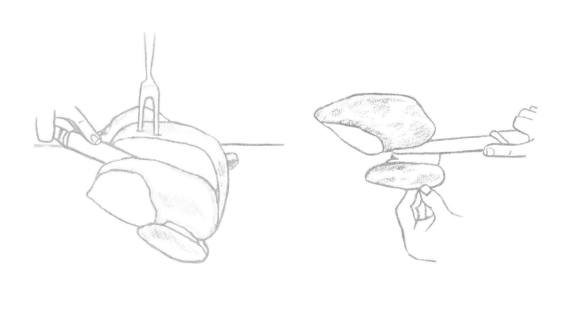

Lightspeed Lemon Chicken
with Garlic and Rosemary

SERVES 4

This recipe produces all the wonderful taste and aroma of a whole roasted chicken in half the time because you're using parts (which cook faster). This sheet pan speedster has turbocharged flavor from the intensity of garlic and rosemary, balanced by the surprising mellow richness of the chicken.

3½ to 4 pounds of your favorite **chicken parts** (see Tips & Tweaks)

1½ tablespoons **extra-virgin olive oil**

2 **garlic cloves**, finely grated (see Garlic Prep, page 13)

Finely grated **zest** of **1 lemon** (optional; see Tips & Tweaks)

2 teaspoons **kosher salt**

Freshly ground black pepper to taste

4 large sprigs **fresh rosemary**, thyme, or sage

Chopped **fresh parsley** or other herbs, for serving

get it set

Heat the oven to 400°F.

Set out all your ingredients.

1. Pat the chicken pieces dry with paper towels. This will help crisp up the skin (damp skin creates steam that could make it rubbery and prevent browning).

2. In a small bowl, mix together the olive oil, garlic, lemon zest if using, salt, and pepper until it turns into a paste. Using your hands, rub the mixture all over the chicken pieces.

3. Place the chicken on a rimmed sheet pan, leaving space between the parts (this helps the air circulate and the chicken brown). Scatter the rosemary sprigs over the chicken. Thoroughly wash your hands and any dishes and surfaces that have been touched by the raw chicken.

4. Roast the chicken until the skin is crisp and golden and the chicken juices run clear when pierced with a knife (see Chicken: Is It Done Yet?, opposite), 20 to 25 minutes for white meat and 25 to 35 minutes for dark meat.

5. Using oven mitts, remove the pan from the oven. Let the chicken sit for 5 minutes so it can reabsorb the juices. Then serve it, garnished with chopped parsley.

● The white meat of a chicken cooks faster than the fattier dark meat. You can roast dark and white parts together on one pan as long as you use tongs to take the white meat out of the oven a few minutes before the dark meat. It can help to group the dark meat on one side of the pan and the white meat on the other. Or, if everyone likes the same cuts, use all white meat (breasts) or all dark meat (drumsticks and thighs), which means all the chicken pieces will be done at the same time.

● Change up the flavor here by spiking the garlic-paste mixture with different seasonings. Replace the lemon zest with a teaspoon of ground spices like cumin, coriander, garam masala (see Rich Blends, page 71), fennel seeds, curry powder, or mustard powder. Or make a milder, more traditional chicken by using the garlic paste alone, without any extra seasoning at all.

chicken: is it done yet?

Chicken is not done cooking until it reaches a temperature of **at least 165°F.** Any lower and it may harbor germs that could make you sick. (This is also why you always have to wash your hands after handling raw chicken, as well as any dishes and surfaces the chicken may have touched.)

There are three ways to make sure your chicken is fully cooked and safe.

1. The most accurate test is to insert an instant-read thermometer into the meat near the inner thigh (between the leg and the breast). Don't let the tip of the thermometer touch a bone, because the bones are hotter than the meat. If you're roasting pieces, take the reading in the thickest part of the largest piece. You need to get it to 165°F.

2. No thermometer? No problem. Use a paring knife to cut into the thigh, piercing to the bone. If you see pink juices or red flesh, put the bird back into the oven.

3. You can also pierce the skin between the leg and the breast with a paring knife to see if the juices are running clear, which indicates that it's cooked through, but this method is less reliable than cutting to the bone.

If you've taken the chicken out of the oven and you see any red or dark pink thigh meat as you carve it, just put it back in the oven to cook a little longer. If the dark meat isn't done but the breast meat is, you can carve the breast meat off the bone (see How to Carve a Chicken, page 108) and return the rest of the chicken to roast for another 10 minutes or so.

Garlicky Chicken on Jammy Tomatoes

SERVES 4

Cherry tomatoes cook down to a rich, savory, jammy bed for this gleaming dark-meat chicken. Cooked together, the flavors meld and shimmer. This recipe is a great way to show off any fresh thyme or oregano you have growing in your garden or on your windowsill, or that you picked up from a farmers' market—just throw some sprigs onto the baking pan before you put it in the oven.

2 tablespoons **extra-virgin olive oil**, plus more for drizzling

1½ tablespoons **cider vinegar** or **fresh lemon juice**, plus more (optional) for serving

2 **garlic cloves**, finely grated (see Garlic Prep, page 13)

1 tablespoon **sweet paprika**

1½ teaspoons **kosher salt**, plus more as needed

1 teaspoon **dried oregano**

½ teaspoon **ground cumin**

3 pounds **bone-in, skin-on chicken drumsticks** and **thighs** (you can use both, or either, or see Tips & Tweaks)

1 pint **cherry tomatoes**, halved

3 or 4 sprigs **fresh oregano** or **thyme** (optional)

¼ cup chopped **fresh parsley** or other herbs, for serving

get it set

Heat the oven to 425°F.

Set out all your ingredients.

1. In a small bowl, stir together the olive oil, cider vinegar, garlic, paprika, salt, oregano, and cumin.

2. Pat the chicken dry with paper towels and place it on a rimmed sheet pan. Pour the paprika mixture over it, turning the pieces to thoroughly coat them. Wash your hands after handling the raw chicken.

3. Add the tomatoes and any herb sprigs to the sheet pan, spreading them out around the chicken. Season the tomatoes lightly with salt and drizzle with a little olive oil.

4. Roast for 15 minutes. Then, using a long-handled spoon, give the tomatoes a stir but don't disturb the chicken. Continue roasting until the chicken is golden and cooked through (the juices will run clear when you pierce a piece with a knife; see Chicken: Is It Done Yet, page 110), 10 to 20 minutes longer (for a total roasting time of 25 to 35 minutes).

5. Transfer the chicken to serving plates. Stir the tomatoes around in the pan, scraping up the delicious browned bits from the bottom of the pan. Stir in the chopped parsley. Taste, and add salt and a drizzle of vinegar if you like. Spoon the tomatoes over the chicken to serve.

tips & tweaks

● You can substitute chicken breasts here. Skin-on, bone-in breasts have the best flavor, and the skin will get nice and crisp in the oven. Boneless, skinless breasts work, too; just reduce the roasting time by 5 minutes. The tomatoes may not get quite as jammy but will still taste great.

● Don't substitute cut-up regular tomatoes for cherry tomatoes. They won't turn as jammy as cherry tomatoes, and they will leak more juices into the pan, which can prevent browning.

Crispy Ginger Chicken Wings

SERVES 4 TO 6 AS A MAIN COURSE, 8 TO 10 AS A PARTY SNACK

Delicious for dinner and perfect for parties, these crispy chicken wings are a little sweet, a little spicy, and extremely, deeply gingery. The only practical way to eat them is with your hands, so have lots of napkins at the ready and be prepared to feast.

1 (2-inch) chunk **fresh ginger,** peeled (see How to Prep Ginger, page 86)

4 **garlic cloves,** peeled (see Garlic Prep, page 13)

½ cup **hoisin sauce**

⅓ cup **soy sauce** or **tamari**

¼ cup **orange juice**

¼ cup **fresh lime juice**

2 tablespoons **honey**

1 tablespoon **Sriracha** or other **hot sauce**

3 pounds **chicken wings,** any wing tips removed

Kosher salt

Toasted (Asian) sesame oil, for drizzling

get it set

Line a rimmed sheet pan with a nonstick liner or parchment paper, and place a metal cooling rack on top of the liner.

Set out all your ingredients.

1. Using a Microplane or other grater, grate the ginger into a large bowl. Without washing the grater, grate the garlic cloves into the same bowl.

2. Add the hoisin sauce, soy sauce, orange juice, lime juice, honey, and Sriracha and mix well.

3. Pat the chicken wings dry with paper towels, then season them lightly all over with salt. Add the wings to the ginger sauce in the bowl, and toss well. Thoroughly wash your hands and any dishes and surfaces that have been touched by the raw chicken. Cover the bowl with a plate or plastic wrap, and refrigerate it for at least 4 hours or overnight to allow the chicken to absorb the flavors of the marinade.

4. When you are ready to cook the wings, heat the oven to 350°F.

5. Arrange the wings in one layer on the rack in the sheet pan. Drizzle with sesame oil. Bake the chicken until it's very tender, 1 to 1½ hours.

6. Turn the broiler on high, and broil the chicken for 1 to 2 minutes to crisp the skin. Serve immediately, with lots of napkins.

Yakitori Chicken

Yakitori is a classic Japanese chicken skewer, often grilled. This version uses rich thigh meat, with lively ginger and garlic flavors that are rounded out with syrupy mirin (a sweet Japanese rice wine) and a touch of sake or sherry to add depth. Serve this as a main course with rice and maybe some sliced cucumbers to catch the sauce. Or make it as an appetizer.

1 pound **boneless, skinless chicken thighs**

½ cup **dark soy sauce** or **tamari**

¼ cup **mirin**

2 tablespoons **sake, dry sherry,** or **dry vermouth** (or use chicken broth)

1 tablespoon **brown sugar**

2 **garlic cloves,** peeled and smashed (see Garlic Prep, page 13)

½ teaspoon grated **fresh ginger** (see How to Prep Ginger, page 86)

Scallions (white and green parts), thinly sliced, for garnish

get it set

Position a rack 4 inches below the broiler element.

If you are using wooden or bamboo skewers, soak them in water for 1 hour; this keeps them from singeing in the broiler (you don't need to do this with metal skewers).

Set out all your ingredients.

1. Cut the chicken into 1-inch pieces and place them in a shallow dish. Wash your hands and the cutting board well.

2. In a small saucepan, combine the soy sauce, mirin, sake, brown sugar, garlic, and ginger. Bring to a simmer and cook for 5 to 7 minutes, until reduced by half.

3. Measure out 2 tablespoons of the sauce and put it in a bowl for serving. Pour the remaining sauce over the chicken. Cover, and chill for at least 1 hour and up to 4 hours so the chicken can absorb the flavors.

4. Heat the broiler to high. Push the chicken pieces onto skewers, leaving a little space between them so the meat can brown. Place the skewers on a rimmed sheet pan and broil for 3 minutes. Using oven mitts, turn the skewers over and broil the other side until the chicken is charred in spots, another 2 to 5 minutes. Serve drizzled with the sauce and garnished with scallions.

tips & tweaks

● You can turn just about anything into yakitori, because this sauce can make most ingredients delicious: • **Tofu,** cut into cubes • **Vegetables,** cut into cubes • **Boneless pork,** cut into chunks • Beef, cut into chunks • **Thick fish like tuna or swordfish,** cut into pieces (this will cook faster than the others)

The timing for all of these will be nearly the same as for the chicken (except for the fish). Watch closely to see when things are nicely browned.

Sticky, Tangy Soy Sauce Chicken

SERVES 6

These Asian-inspired chicken thighs get sweet from honey and snappy from ginger, lime, and soy sauce. The dark meat of the thighs has a deep savory flavor that balances the tangy sauce. Serve these with fluffy white rice, crisp lettuce, or other vegetables. This is a sticky one, so have extra napkins ready.

1 to 2 **limes**

1 large **garlic clove,** peeled (see Garlic Prep, page 13)

1 (1-inch) chunk **fresh ginger,** peeled (see How to Prep Ginger, page 86)

2½ tablespoons **Asian fish sauce**

2 tablespoons **soy sauce**

2 tablespoons **honey**

1 tablespoon **toasted (Asian) sesame oil**

Pinch of **crushed red pepper flakes** (optional)

2½ pounds **boneless, skinless chicken thighs**

Kosher salt and **freshly ground black pepper**

Handful of **fresh cilantro leaves** and tender stems, for serving

Lettuce leaves, such as Bibb or romaine, or cooked rice, for serving

get it set

Heat the oven to 425°F.

Set out all your ingredients.

1. Using a Microplane or other grater, grate 1 teaspoon lime zest. Cut the limes in half and squeeze out 1 tablespoon of juice.

2. Place lime juice and zest in a large bowl. Using that same grater (you don't need to wash it), grate the garlic and ginger into the bowl. Mix in the fish sauce, soy sauce, honey, sesame oil, and red pepper flakes if using.

3. Pat the chicken thighs dry with paper towels. Sprinkle them lightly with salt (you don't need much because the soy sauce already has plenty). Add the chicken to the bowl and turn to coat well with the soy sauce mixture. If you have time, let the chicken sit for 10 to 15 minutes to marinate (this gives the chicken a deeper flavor, but you can skip this step). Arrange the chicken pieces on a rimmed sheet pan and pour the sauce over them. Thoroughly wash your hands and any dishes and surfaces that have been touched by the raw chicken.

4. Roast the chicken for 15 minutes. Then use tongs to flip the pieces. Continue roasting until the chicken is browned and caramelized, another 15 to 20 minutes (total roasting time will be 30 to 35 minutes).

5. Top chicken with black pepper and sprinkle with cilantro or other herbs. Serve over lettuce or rice.

tips & tweaks

● You can substitute boneless, skinless chicken breasts for the thighs. Just cook them for about 5 minutes less.

Sausage + Peppers 4^{ever}

Complicated and wonderful chemical changes occur when you roast a bell pepper: It softens and caramelizes, which brings out its inner sugars and makes it sweeter. Now combine this with the savory pop of sausages and you get that other chemical reaction, which taste-bud scientists call "deliciousness." This concoction is particularly excellent over mashed potatoes.

2 **sweet bell peppers** (red, orange, yellow, or a combination), halved, seeds and stems removed, sliced into ¼-inch-wide strips

1 small **red onion,** sliced into ¼-inch-thick rounds

1½ tablespoons **extra-virgin olive oil**

¾ teaspoon **kosher salt,** plus more as needed

Freshly ground black pepper, as needed

4 **fresh sausages** (about 1 pound), any kind you like (see Tips & Tweaks), each pricked in four places with a fork

½ teaspoon **red wine vinegar** or **cider vinegar,** plus more as needed

1 tablespoon finely chopped **fresh basil, mint,** or other herb

get it set

Heat the oven to 400°F.

Set out all your ingredients.

1. Put the pepper and onion slices on a large rimmed sheet pan and toss with the oil, salt, and black pepper. Spread the vegetables out into a single layer. Roast until soft but not caramelized (see Browning: How Heat Creates Flavor, page 236), about 10 minutes.

2. Using tongs, put the sausages on top of the vegetables. Continue roasting until the peppers caramelize and the sausages are cooked through, 20 to 25 minutes.

3. To serve, transfer the sausages to plates, leaving the peppers and onions in the sheet pan. Toss the peppers and onions with the vinegar and basil. Taste, and add more vinegar, if needed. Serve over the sausages.

tips & tweaks	● Use your favorite kind of sausages here—anything from sweet Italian to chorizo to chicken with sun-dried tomato. Just be sure to get fresh sausages meant for cooking, not the cured kind that have been dried, like salami. Precooked fresh sausages, like bratwurst and kielbasa, are also fine to use, as are vegan or meatless sausages. Peppers get along with everyone.

Melting Buttery Salmon

Salmon is an easy fish to love: it's not "fishy," and cooked gently it has a sweetly mellow taste, whose full charm wakes up with a touch of lemon. This is simple to make, yet on the plate with melting butter it reads fancy. To gussy it up even more, see the Salmon Mood Board, opposite, for lots of variations. This is a perfect but basic recipe that you can make your own with a personal spin.

1 **lemon**

4 (6- to 8-ounce) **skinless salmon fillets** (see Tips & Tweaks)

1 **garlic clove**, finely grated (see Garlic Prep, page 13)

Kosher salt, as needed

3 tablespoons / 45 grams **unsalted butter**, cut into small cubes

Freshly ground black pepper

Chopped **fresh herbs**, for serving

Lemon wedges, for serving

get it set

Heat the oven to 300°F.

Set out all your ingredients.

1. Cut 4 thin slices from the lemon and poke out the seeds. Cut the rest of the lemon into wedges to use later.

2. Place the salmon on a rimmed sheet pan or in a 9 x 13-inch baking dish. Rub the grated garlic evenly over the tops of the salmon pieces. Sprinkle the salmon lightly with salt. Top each salmon fillet with a lemon slice and a few pieces of butter.

3. Bake the salmon until it's just cooked through, 15 to 25 minutes, depending on how thick the pieces are. (Use a fork to poke one of the salmon pieces to check. It should look dark pink and should be tender but not flaky–that's overcooked.)

4. Use a spatula to transfer the salmon to plates. Squeeze some of the lemon wedges into the butter remaining in the sheet pan (do this to taste). Using a spoon, distribute this lemony butter over the salmon. Top each fillet with black pepper and chopped herbs. Serve with lemon wedges.

salmon mood board

how do I feel today?

saucy

Serve with (choose one)

Chunky Cherry Tomato Salsa, page 61

Pesto, page 93

Sriracha

Soy dipping sauce, page 203

Mayonnaise spiked with mustard

spicy

Sprinkle with ground spices before baking (choose one)

Paprika

Cumin

Coriander

Curry powder

Garam masala (see Rich Blends, page 71)

Turmeric

Chile powder

tart

Use a dash of vinegar instead of lemon wedges (choose one)

Cider vinegar

Balsamic vinegar

Sherry vinegar

Wine vinegar, red or white

Rice vinegar

fresh

Add some herbs to the pan (choose one or two)

Thyme

Tarragon

Rosemary

Sage

Bay leaf

Or sprinkle herbs on top after cooking (choose one or even a few)

Mint

Basil

Cilantro

Dill

Parsley

tips & tweaks

● Salmon fillets are sold in different thicknesses depending upon the size of the fish and whether they're cut from the thin tail end or the thick belly. Always try to get fillets that are the same thickness so they cook at the same rate. Otherwise, thick ones will take longer than thin ones.

● This basic fish cooking technique will work for any kind of fish fillets or steaks you've got: cod, tilapia, mackerel, hake, tuna. Just keep in mind that the thicker the piece of fish, the longer it will take to cook.

● Baking the fish at a relatively low temperature keeps it juicy and tender, and makes it easier to catch it before it overcooks.

● Got leftovers? They go great in a grain bowl like the Heavenly Bowl (page 139) or on top of a salad.

Unmistakably Herby Meatballs

Meatballs know who they are. A meatball is a meatball no matter what it's made of, and isn't that what we love about it? Combine any ground meat with garlic, herbs, and spices, roll it into a ball, and you have a super-flavorful dish in itself, or you can nestle a few in a pita, or heap them on pasta with tomato sauce (see page 90). Broiling on a sheet pan is easier and quicker than frying, and it heats more evenly, so this lovable meatball is also a snap to make.

1 large **egg**

1 pound **ground meat** (beef, turkey, chicken, pork, lamb—you name it)

½ cup **plain bread crumbs**

¼ cup **minced onion** (see Onion Prep, page 12) or scallions (white and green parts)

1 teaspoon **kosher salt**

¼ teaspoon **freshly ground black pepper**

1 or 2 **garlic cloves**, finely grated (see Garlic Prep, page 13)

2 tablespoons chopped **fresh parsley, mint, cilantro,** or other fresh herbs

Olive oil, for drizzling

seasoning mixes

Middle Eastern (use any or all of the following): 2 teaspoons **cumin seeds** or 1 teaspoon ground cumin • ½ teaspoon **chile powder** or 1 pinch of cayenne pepper • ½ teaspoon **ground cinnamon** • ¼ teaspoon **ground allspice**

Italian (perfect for spaghetti and meatballs): ½ cup / 50 grams grated **Parmesan cheese** • 1 teaspoon **dried oregano** • ¼ teaspoon freshly grated **nutmeg**

get it set

Position a rack 4 inches below the broiler element and heat the broiler.

Set out all your ingredients.

1. Crack the egg into a large bowl and use a fork to mix it until the yolk and white are well combined.

2. Add the meat, bread crumbs, onions, salt, pepper, garlic, and chopped parsley or other herbs to the egg in the bowl. Add any seasoning mixes, if using. Use your clean hands or a flexible spatula to gently mix everything together, but don't overwork the mixture or the meatballs will be tough. Stop when the herbs look evenly distributed into the meat.

3. Using your hands, form the meat mixture into 1½-inch balls, and place them on a rimmed sheet pan. Drizzle each meatball with a little olive oil.

4. Broil until the meatballs are browned on top and cooked through in the center (cut into one to check), 7 to 12 minutes–you don't need to turn them. Serve 'em up hot or warm.

All Together Now Kebabs

With its succulent morsels of beef or lamb, this dish is on point. I like the Middle Eastern–inspired mix of allspice, cinnamon, and cumin in the recipe, but you should feel free to tweak the heck out of it (see Tips & Tweaks). These are fabulous with garlicky yogurt for dunking, or with the tahini sauce on page 136.

2 tablespoons **extra-virgin olive oil**

2 **garlic cloves**, finely grated (see Garlic Prep, page 13)

1 teaspoon **kosher salt**, plus a pinch

½ teaspoon **ground cumin**

½ teaspoon **ground paprika**

½ teaspoon **ground cinnamon**

¼ teaspoon **ground allspice**

¼ teaspoon **freshly ground black pepper**

Pinch of **cayenne pepper** (optional)

1 pound **boneless beef** or **lamb**, cut into 1½-inch cubes

1 cup **plain yogurt** or sour cream

1 tablespoon chopped **fresh cilantro** or **mint**, or a combination

1 large **red onion**, cut into 1½-inch chunks

Lemon wedges, for serving

get it set

If you are using wooden or bamboo skewers, soak them in water for 1 hour; this keeps them from singeing under the broiler (you don't need to do this with metal skewers).

Set a rack 4 inches below the broiler element.

Set out all your ingredients.

Line a rimmed sheet pan with foil (optional).

1. In a large bowl, mix together the oil, half of the grated garlic, the salt, cumin, paprika, cinnamon, allspice, black pepper, and cayenne if using. Add the meat and toss well to coat the pieces. Let the meat marinate for at least 30 minutes at room temperature or up to 24 hours in the refrigerator.

2. To make the sauce, in a small bowl, mix together the yogurt, a pinch of salt, the remaining grated garlic, and the cilantro or mint. Set it aside for serving.

3. When you are ready to cook, heat the broiler.

4. Thread the meat and onions onto skewers (use 4 skewers for 4 servings), pressing the pieces up next to each other. Place the skewers on the sheet pan. Broil until the tops are browned and slightly charred, 3 to 4 minutes. Using oven mitts, flip the skewers over and continue broiling until the meat is browned and charred at the edges on the other side, but still rare or medium-rare inside (or medium if you must), another 2 to 4 minutes.

5. Serve the skewers with the yogurt sauce and lemon wedges.

**tips &
tweaks**

● Here's a secret: You don't really need the skewers. Yes, for grilling they are essential to keep the meat from falling into the fire. But when you broil, skewers are merely convenient for moving the meat. If you don't have skewers, just spread the meat cubes out on the pan and broil as directed.

● Play with the seasonings. Instead of the Middle Eastern–inspired combination in the recipe, substitute other spices or dried (not fresh) herbs:

- Garam masala (see Rich Blends, page 71)
- Coriander
- Turmeric
- Ginger
- Oregano
- Thyme
- Rosemary

Secret Ingredient Tofu
with Obvious Broccoli

SERVES 4

You can keep a secret, right? *Shh. It's ketchup!* That's what makes this so easy and so good, like barbecued chicken but meatless. If you think you don't like tofu, this is the dish to convert you (and if it doesn't, well, try the awesome chicken variation in the Tips & Tweaks section). The ketchup mixture makes this mysteriously delicious, and the broccoli adds an easily identified crunch. So now you know.

1 (14- to 16-ounce) package **firm tofu**, drained (see Tips & Tweaks, page 128)

1 large head of **broccoli** (trim off the bottom of the stem if it looks brown)

5 tablespoons **grapeseed** or **sunflower oil**, divided, plus more for the pan

2 **garlic cloves**, finely grated (see Garlic Prep, page 13)

⅓ cup **ketchup**

2 tablespoons **soy sauce**

2 tablespoons **Asian fish sauce**

Pinch of **cayenne pepper**

¼ teaspoon **salt**

1 **lime**, halved

Cooked white rice, for serving

get it set

Heat the oven to 425°F.

Set out all your ingredients.

Oil a rimmed sheet pan.

1. Wrap the tofu in a clean kitchen towel or paper towels, and place it on a plate. Top it with a second plate and put something heavy, like a can of beans, on top to weight it down. Leave it while you cut the broccoli and make the sauce. This will remove some of the moisture from the tofu, which lets it absorb the maximum amount of sauce.

2. Cut the broccoli, including the stem, into bite-size pieces and set aside.

3. In a small pot, heat 3 tablespoons of the oil over medium heat. Add the garlic and cook, stirring it around a few times, until it is just starting to turn golden, about 1 minute. Keep an eye on it–garlic burns really quickly. If it starts to get too brown, pull the pan off the heat for a few seconds to cool it down.

4. Stir in the ketchup (carefully–it might splatter when it first goes into the pot), soy sauce, fish sauce, and cayenne. Bring to

(recipe continues)

a simmer and cook, stirring, for 2 minutes to thicken the mixture slightly. Set the sauce aside.

5. Unwrap the tofu and cut it in half lengthwise. Slice the halves crosswise into ½-inch-thick slabs so you have nice chunky cubes.

6. Place the tofu cubes in an even layer on the oiled sheet pan, leaving a little space around each piece so the heat circulates evenly and crisps the tofu. Brush with the sauce, then flip the tofu over and brush the other side.

7. Place the broccoli in a bowl and toss with the remaining 2 tablespoons oil and the salt. Scatter the broccoli around the tofu on the pan. Roast everything together until the broccoli is cooked through (it should be tender when you stab it with a fork) and starting to brown, about 20 minutes. Squeeze the lime halves over everything right after you take the pan out (when they are still hot, the broccoli and tofu will absorb the maximum flavor and brightness from the lime juice). Serve hot, with the rice on the side.

tips & tweaks

● Not into tofu? Try this with 1 pound of boneless, skinless chicken breasts, cut into 1½-inch pieces. You don't need to weight them down under a can the way you do the tofu—just cut them up, toss with the sauce, and cook as directed in the recipe. See Chicken: Is It Done Yet?, page 110.

choose the right tofu

Tofu is made from mashed soybeans that are pressed into a block or pillow. Soybeans have a high water content, and the more water pressed out of them when the plant is processed, the firmer the resulting tofu.

● **Soft tofu** is mild and milky, and has a jiggly, delicate consistency like Jell-O. It's a great base for desserts, but it doesn't fry well.

● **Medium-firm tofu** has a denser texture but it's still pretty fragile. It's a good choice when braising or boiling, where you don't have to move it around much. This is what you find in miso soup.

● **Firm tofu** is the most versatile. It contains little water, making it great for panfrying, baking, and boiling. It holds its shape nicely, but it's porous enough to absorb lots of flavors.

● **Extra-firm tofu** has tight soybean curds and its texture has the most chew. It's used for heartier dishes like tofu steak.

● **Silken tofu** is not pressed at all, staying soft and silky with a texture almost like thick yogurt or pudding. Silken tofu is the perfect ingredient for smoothies, "creamy" sauces like dressings, and mayonnaises, and it makes for a good vegan whipped cream.

Coconut Roasted Sweet Potatoes + Chickpeas

Roasting sweet potatoes brings out their gorgeous, deep flavor like nothing else. Right from the oven, they're almost too good to do anything to them, and yet adding mellow chickpeas and sweet coconut brings out an unexpected extra dimension. Cinnamon and garam masala give it an earthy depth, and tomato paste adds an umami richness. It's a colorful, spicy vegetarian meal that covers all the bases.

1 pound **sweet potatoes**, peeled and cut into 1-inch chunks

3½ tablespoons **extra-virgin olive oil**, divided, plus more for serving (optional)

1 small **shallot**, thinly sliced

1 teaspoon packed **light brown sugar**

Kosher salt

¼ teaspoon **freshly ground black pepper**

3 or 4 **cinnamon sticks**

3 to 5 sprigs **fresh thyme**, rosemary, or sage

1½ tablespoons **tomato paste**

2 teaspoons **garam masala** or **curry powder** (see Rich Blends, page 71)

Pinch of **cayenne pepper** (optional)

2 (15-ounce) cans **chickpeas**, drained and rinsed

½ cup **unsweetened coconut milk** (freeze the rest of the can for up to 6 months)

2 teaspoons **fresh lime juice**, or more to taste

2 tablespoons diced **red onion** (see Onion Prep, page 12)

½ cup chopped **fresh cilantro leaves** and tender stems

get it set

Heat the oven to 350°F.

Set out all your ingredients.

1. In a medium bowl, toss together the sweet potatoes, 1 tablespoon of the olive oil, the shallot, brown sugar, a large pinch of salt, and the black pepper.

2. Spread the sweet potatoes in an even layer on a large rimmed sheet pan. Tuck the cinnamon sticks and thyme sprigs around the potatoes. Bake the potatoes for 30 minutes, tossing them once or twice.

3. While the sweet potatoes are baking, in the same bowl you used for the potatoes (you don't need to wash it), whisk together the tomato paste, garam masala, cayenne if using, 1½ tablespoons of the olive oil, and ¾ teaspoon salt. Fold in the chickpeas until evenly coated.

(recipe continues)

4. When the sweet potatoes have baked for 30 minutes, raise the oven temperature to 400°F. Add the chickpeas to the sheet pan, scattering them around the sweet potatoes, and roast, tossing halfway through, until everything is soft and caramelized, about 15 minutes. Using oven mitts, remove the sheet pan from the oven.

5. In a small bowl, whisk together the coconut milk, lime juice, and the remaining 1 tablespoon olive oil.

6. Using tongs, pluck the thyme sprigs and cinnamon sticks from the sheet pan and discard them. Sprinkle the red onion and cilantro over the chickpeas and sweet potatoes, and drizzle everything with the coconut milk mixture. Toss well, and season to taste, adding more salt and lime juice as needed. Drizzle with more olive oil for serving, if you'd like.

INSTEAD OF . . .	USE . . .
sweet potatoes	cubed butternut squash
chickpeas	canned white beans
1 tablespoon of olive oil in Step 1	1 tablespoon of coconut oil (but use olive oil in Step 5 because it adds a welcome savor to the sauce)

some tasty swaps

Extreme Bowling

grain bowls & salads

Grain Bowl Basics

Want to use up some leftovers and make a work of art at the same time? Enter the grain bowl! Grain bowls are easy to put together, hard to get wrong, and have a mix of flavors and textures that are infinitely variable and delicious. Plus, bowls make leftovers feel new and are insanely good for you. Yes, grain bowls are all that.

Use the recipes that follow for practice and inspiration, then improvise your own bowls using the chart opposite. Once you know the basic structure, you can't go wrong.

Grains may be the main ingredient, but they're not the star of the show. They're really the backdrop, providing earthiness and texture.

Vegetables form the basic flavors of your bowl. Something green for freshness, something raw for crunch. Leftover roasted veggies work great, too.

Proteins add heft to your bowl. One is usually enough. Any leftover meats, fish, or tofu are great—or take a sec and sear something on top of the stove. An egg works, too. The runny yolk of a poached egg coats the other ingredients like a sauce.

Sauce pulls it all together. A perfect sauce melds with the other flavors and brings out something new in them, usually because of the tang of an acid.

Garnish gives your dish an exciting initial taste or texture, or even just a shot of color, that sets the whole bowl off from the start.

The Epic Grain Bowl

VEGETABLES
(choose as many as you want)

SAUCES
(choose 1)

LISTED FROM LIGHTER TO HEARTIER:

White rice

Quinoa

Fonio

Bulgur

Brown rice

Einkorn

Farro

Kamut

Wheat berries

GRAINS

GREENS:

Fresh kale

Sautéed spinach

Collards

ROASTED:

Zucchini

Eggplant

Tomatoes

Sweet potato

Mushrooms

RAW, FOR CONTRAST & CRUNCH:

Radish

Cucumber

Fennel

Sugar snap peas

Carrots

LEFTOVERS OR FRESHLY COOKED:

Meats

Fish

Tofu

Beans

PERSONAL FAVES:

Poached egg

Jammy egg

PROTEINS

(choose 1 or 2, max)

Lemony Tahini Dressing (page 136)

Soy sauce, rice vinegar, sesame oil, and a little ginger (page 203)

Sesame Lime Dressing (page 141)

Basic mustard vinaigrette (page 146)

Caesar Dressing (page 149)

Yogurt sauce (page 139)

Buttermilk Ranch Dressing (page 152)

PUNGENT/ SPICY:

Kimchi

Onions prepared as Veggie Quick Pickles (page 67)

Pickled jalapeño (page 48)

CRUNCHY:

Toasted nuts

Toasted seeds

COLORFUL:

Fresh herbs

GARNISHES

(choose 1 or 2)

Harmony Bowl

Lemony Tahini, Quinoa & Roasted Veggies

Lemony Tahini Dressing is what brings this bowl together. The lemon will highlight the flavors of whatever vegetables you use, and the creamy texture makes the ingredients feel melty and rich. Substitute any vegetable you like here—just keep some crunch involved. This sauce is also a great salad dressing or dip if you have some left over . . . not that you'll have any left over.

lemony tahini dressing

2 tablespoons **fresh lemon juice**

1 **garlic clove**, finely grated or minced (see Garlic Prep, page 13)

¼ teaspoon **kosher salt**

¼ cup **extra-virgin olive oil**

3 tablespoons **tahini**

grain bowl

1 pound **brussels sprouts**, ends trimmed, any yellowing outer leaves removed (sprouts halved if they're larger than 1 inch)

1½ pounds **carrots** or **butternut squash**, peeled and cut into 1-inch chunks

Extra-virgin olive oil, as needed

Kosher salt

1 cup **quinoa**

2 tablespoons **fresh lemon juice**

1 tablespoon **honey** or agave syrup

Large pinch of **crushed red pepper flakes**, plus more for garnish

1 cup **cherry tomatoes,** quartered

Fresh mint, basil, or **cilantro leaves**, for garnish

get it set

Heat the oven to 425°F.

Set out all your ingredients.

1. Make the Lemony Tahini Dressing: In a medium bowl, whisk the lemon juice, garlic, and salt. Let sit for 1 minute to let the salt dissolve and the garlic mellow in the lemon juice. Slowly whisk in the oil, a few drops at a time, until the mixture is smooth. Whisk in the tahini and enough water (add it teaspoon by teaspoon) to make a thin, pourable sauce; set aside.

2. Put the bowl together: Place the brussels sprouts on one rimmed sheet pan and the carrots on another. Toss all the vegetables with just enough olive oil and a sprinkle of salt to coat them. Roast the vegetables, tossing them once or twice, until they are browned and tender: 17 to 22 minutes for the brussels sprouts, 20 to 30 minutes for the carrots.

3. While the vegetables are in the oven, cook the quinoa: In a medium saucepan, combine the quinoa with 2 cups of water and ¼ teaspoon salt. Bring to a boil, then reduce it to a simmer and cook for 15 minutes, until the grains soften and the water is absorbed. Transfer the quinoa to a medium bowl and set it aside.

4. In a small bowl, whisk together the lemon juice, honey, ¼ teaspoon salt, and the red pepper flakes. As soon as the carrots or squash are done, toss with the lemon-honey mixture to coat.

5. To serve, divide the quinoa among four bowls. Arrange the brussels sprouts, carrots, and tomatoes in separate mounds on top. Generously drizzle the Lemony Tahini Dressing over the vegetables and garnish with mint leaves and more red pepper flakes.

Heavenly Bowl

SERVES 4

Green Goddess, Grains & Greens

A yogurt-based green goddess dressing on kale, asparagus, and peas, plus plenty of herbs, makes for a heavenly green grain bowl experience. If you have leftovers from Melting Buttery Salmon (page 120) or any of the roast chicken recipes (pages 106 to 113), add them here to make this extra satisfying. The bright herby dressing goes well with any salad greens, or as a dip.

yogurt green goddess dressing

1 cup **plain yogurt,** preferably whole milk (see Tips & Tweaks, page 140)

¼ cup **extra-virgin olive oil**

¾ cup packed soft **fresh herb leaves** or sprigs, such as basil, parsley, mint, or dill, plus more for garnish

2 **garlic cloves,** peeled (see Garlic Prep, page 13)

2 **oil-packed anchovy fillets** (optional)

1 **scallion** (white and green parts), coarsely chopped

1 tablespoon **fresh lime juice,** plus more to taste

Kosher salt and **freshly ground black pepper**

grain bowl

4 ounces **asparagus**

1 large bunch **kale** (about 1 pound)

1 cup **peas,** fresh or frozen (you don't have to thaw them)

4 cups **cooked brown rice** (still warm, or warmed up in the microwave)

8 ounces **cooked salmon** or **chicken** (optional)

Thinly sliced **radishes** or **celery** (or both), with some of the celery leaves if you've got them

get it set

Set out all your ingredients.

1. Make the Yogurt Green Goddess Dressing: In a blender, combine the yogurt, oil, herbs, garlic, anchovies if using, scallion, lime juice, and a pinch each of salt and pepper, and puree until smooth. Taste, and add more salt if it needs it and more lime juice if you want a brighter flavor. Set aside.

2. Put the bowl together: Hold an asparagus spear in your hand and snap off the bottom inch or so. As you bend it, you'll feel the place it wants to break; go with that. Discard the bottom, which is woody, and slice the rest of the spear into 1-inch pieces. Repeat with the remaining spears.

3. Rinse the kale well in a colander. Remove the stem and any thick center ribs from the leaves. Chop the leaves into 2-inch pieces.

(recipe continues)

4. Fill a medium pot with 1 inch of water and place a steamer basket in the bottom of the pot. Bring the water to a simmer, add the kale and asparagus, and cover the pot. Let the vegetables steam for 5 minutes. Then add the peas, placing them on top of the other vegetables, cover again, and continue to steam until everything is tender, 3 to 4 minutes. Use a slotted spoon to transfer the vegetables to a bowl.

5. Divide the brown rice among four serving bowls. Arrange the kale, asparagus, peas, and any salmon or chicken you'd like to add on top. Drizzle each bowl generously with the dressing, and garnish with radishes and/or celery and more herbs.

tips & tweaks

● If you only have Greek yogurt in the fridge, you can use it; just thin it out with a little milk. Otherwise the dressing will be too thick to pour.

● For a completely different take on this, skip the green goddess dressing and substitute the soy sauce–based dressing on page 203. It gives the bowl an Asian vibe that's tart, zesty, salty, and sweet.

● You can substitute spinach for the kale. But since it cooks more quickly than kale, add it later, along with the peas after the asparagus has cooked for 5 minutes. You'll need 5 to 6 ounces of spinach.

Hearty Bowl

Farro, Broccoli & Jammy Eggs

Farro's earthy taste and hearty texture make this an especially satisfying bowl. The citrus sesame dressing adds a zesty bite to crunchy broccoli and carrots, but a soft-yolked egg keeps everything mellow. The farro and the eggs are simmered in the same pot, making this super-simple and streamlined.

grain bowl

Kosher salt, as needed

1½ cups **farro**, rinsed

4 large **eggs**, shells scrubbed under hot running water (see Tips & Tweaks, page 142)

1 large head **broccoli**, cut into florets, with tender stems sliced (about 1¼ pounds)

2 tablespoons **extra-virgin olive oil**, plus more for drizzling

1 teaspoon **soy sauce**, plus more for serving if you like

2 tablespoons **toasted (Asian) sesame oil**

1 tablespoon **sesame seeds**, plus more for serving

Thinly sliced **carrots** or **radishes**, for serving (optional)

1 **scallion** (white and green parts), thinly sliced

Hot sauce or thinly sliced green chiles, for serving (optional)

sesame lime dressing

¼ cup **fresh lime juice** (2 to 3 limes)

3 tablespoons **Asian fish sauce**

2 teaspoons **light brown sugar**

2 tablespoons **toasted (Asian) sesame oil**

get it set

Heat the oven to 450°F.

Put a bowl of ice water next to the stove.

Set out all your ingredients.

1. Start the grain bowl: Bring a medium pot of salted water to a boil. Add the farro and the eggs. Cook the eggs for about 6 minutes for very runny centers or 7 minutes for medium-runny, then use a slotted spoon to transfer the eggs to the bowl of ice water. Let them sit for 2 minutes, then crack and carefully peel the eggs (see Egg Academy, page 30).

2. Continue to cook the farro until it's done according to the package directions, usually a total cooking time of 20 to 40 minutes. Drain the farro in a strainer in the sink.

3. While the farro is cooking, prepare the **Sesame Lime Dressing**: In a medium bowl, whisk together lime juice, fish sauce, and brown sugar. Let it sit for 1 minute to allow the sugar to start dissolving, then slowly whisk in the sesame oil. Set the dressing aside.

(recipe continues)

4. On a rimmed sheet pan, toss the broccoli with the olive oil and soy sauce, then spread the pieces out in an even layer. Roast until the broccoli is tender and browned in spots, 8 to 15 minutes. Let it cool slightly, then toss it with the sesame oil and sesame seeds.

5. In a bowl, toss the drained farro with 2 or 3 tablespoons of the Sesame Lime Dressing, a large pinch of salt, and a drizzle of olive oil.

6. To serve, divide the farro among four serving bowls. Top each serving with carrots, broccoli, and an egg, and garnish with sliced scallions and more sesame seeds. Serve immediately, with the remaining dressing and the hot sauce or sliced chiles, if using, on the side.

tips & tweaks

● Because the eggs are cooked in the same pot as the farro, wash them in hot water before adding them to the pot. This gets rid of anything that might be stuck to the shell—which, if your eggs are from the farmers' market, might include feathers or dirt.

● Different brands of farro have different cooking times because of the way the grains are processed. The more of the natural bran grains that has been removed, the more quickly the grains will cook. Most farro in the United States has been pearled (like barley), meaning all or nearly all of the bran has been stripped away. Pearled farro will cook in about 20 minutes. But you'll sometimes see semipearled (meaning about half of the bran remains) or whole farro (meaning all of the bran is intact). These take longer to cook and have a nuttier, chewier texture. Different varieties and brands have different cooking times, so check the package directions to get a sense of the timing.

● If you use leftover cooked grain for this bowl (brown rice works well), either warm it or let it come to room temperature, and cook the eggs in boiling water for 6 or 7 minutes as described.

Salad Bowl Basics

If your hunger has never been satisfied by a salad, it might mean your salads are just too small. When it comes to salad, I like to think big and varied. Like a grain bowl, a salad is easy to put together and hard to do wrong. I love to mix and match greens, fruits and vegetables, proteins, and starches. Then there are the dressings and toppings.

You can layer up to eight different ingredients in a salad bowl before the bowl gets crowded and confusing. Fewer than three or four, and we're talking a side salad or a light salad—not that there's anything wrong with that. Use what you've got to create a nice mix of textures, colors, shapes, and flavors.

Start with **salad greens**. All lettuces, unless they come in a package that says "triple washed," need a good rinse. See How to Wash & Dry Salad Greens, page 150.

Vegetables & fruits add vibrant flavor to your salads, as well as varied texture and a nice shot of color. Add one or two fruits or veggies. Leftover veggies can be fantastic in fresh salads.

Proteins bring flavor and heft. A little goes a long way, so use just one or two. Leftover proteins from other meals can start a new life in a salad.

Starches in salads can be light and classic, like croutons, while grains, tubers, and squash can bulk up the salad into a main course. (The difference between Salad World and Planet Grain Bowl gets a little blurry at this point, but that's why they're in the same chapter.)

Dressings should match the sturdiness of the greens. Sturdy greens need substantial dressings, like those blended with mayo, yogurt, buttermilk, tahini, or cheese, to help bind all the strong flavors together. And soft greens work best with oil and vinegar or citrus juice–based dressings.

Toppings add a graceful note to a well-composed salad. Most are best sprinkled on top of a salad after it's been dressed and tossed so they don't get soggy or crushed.

The Salad Saga

GREENS

(choose 1, or mix)

CRUNCHY & MILD-TASTING ALL-PURPOSE:

Iceberg
Romaine
Red leaf
Green leaf

SWEET & LIGHT:

Baby lettuces
Butterhead
Bibb
Mesclun

PEPPERY, OR MUSTARDY SPICY:

Arugula
Radicchio
Watercress
Frisée

STURDY, THICK
(mineral rich with a strong vegetal taste; they don't wilt):

Kale
Spinach
Collards
Swiss chard

RAW & SLICED THIN:

Apples
Bell peppers
Celery
Carrots
Cucumbers
Fennel
Onions
Pears
Radishes
Snap peas
Tomatoes
Zucchini

CUT INTO BITE-SIZE PIECES:

Figs
Grapes
Melons
Peaches
Plums

STEAMED OR ROASTED UNTIL TENDER, & CUT INTO BITE-SIZE PIECES:

Asparagus
Beets
Broccoli
Cauliflower
String beans

VEGETABLES & FRUITS

(choose 1 or 2)

PROTEINS

(choose 1 or 2, max)

LEFTOVERS OR FRESHLY COOKED:

Grilled chicken or steak
Roasted chicken or steak
Poached or canned fish*
Country ham
Chorizo
Bacon
Tofu*
Cheese
Beans (any kind)
Chickpeas
Lentils
Hard-boiled egg
Soft-boiled egg

* Add as a topper after salad is dressed and tossed so ingredient doesn't fall apart

STARCHES

Croutons
Quinoa
Farro
Bulgur wheat
Barley
Roasted or boiled potatoes
Roasted sweet potatoes

(choose 1)

DRESSINGS

(choose the right match; see opposite)

FOR ANY GREENS, ESPECIALLY SOFT OR LIGHT GREENS:

Any vinaigrette such as Mustard Vinaigrette (page 146)
Sesame Lime Dressing (page 141)

FOR ANY EXCEPT LIGHT GREENS:

Caesar Dressing (page 149)
Yogurt Green Goddess Dressing (page 139)
Buttermilk Ranch Dressing (page 152)

FOR STURDY GREENS:

Any dressing blended with mayo, yogurt, buttermilk, tahini, or cheese

TOPPINGS

(choose 1 or 2)

TOPPINGS THAT POP:

Pumpkin seeds
Bacon
Cheese
Fresh herbs
Olives

NO-TOSS TOPPERS
(to add after salad is dressed & tossed):

Croutons
Roasted chickpeas
Toasted nuts
Dried fruit
Sliced avocado
Fresh berries

Always in the Fridge Mustard Vinaigrette

MAKES ⅔ CUP, ENOUGH TO DRESS 4 TO 6 SALADS

Salad dressings, like salad itself, take a few elements and create endless variety. A basic dressing is made only of oil (like olive oil), an acid (like lemon juice or vinegar), and salt (like, you know, salt). This one also has mustard for depth. Keep this vinaigrette on hand and making salads will be a breeze.

3 tablespoons **vinegar** (red wine, white wine, balsamic, rice, and cider are good ones), or more to taste

1 teaspoon **Dijon mustard**

½ teaspoon **fine sea salt**, or more to taste

Large pinch of **freshly ground black pepper**

½ cup **extra-virgin olive oil**

get it set

Take out a jar with a tight-fitting lid.

Set out all your ingredients.

1. Put the vinegar, mustard, salt, and pepper in the jar, cover, and shake well for 20 seconds to dissolve the salt.

2. Add the olive oil, cover the jar, and shake for another 20 seconds, until it looks thick and well mixed. Taste, and add a little more vinegar if it tastes flat or salt if it needs it, shaking after each addition. Use immediately or store in the refrigerator for up a month–in the same container you made it in! Shake well before using.

don't overdress

Always start with less dressing than you think you'll need, because you can't un-dress a salad. Taste a leaf after each drizzle to test, then add another drizzle if necessary and toss. Repeat until the salad is perfectly dressed.

tips & tweaks

● The oil may solidify in the fridge, but that's just oil being oil. Shaking the jar vigorously before using it will help melt the oil.

● The key to this vinaigrette's long fridge life is that it uses only a few stable ingredients. Once you start adding fresh herbs, garlic, or lemon juice, those flavors will fade sooner. So use it up in about a week.

Are you stuck with only one salad dressing for eternity? No, of course not!
Vinaigrettes can morph any which way!

The Shapeshifter Vinaigrette

If you take out the _____ . . .

. . . you can replace it with _____ instead.
(choose one)

If you take out the . . .	. . . you can replace it with _____ instead. (choose one)
dijon mustard	Whole-grain mustard Honey mustard No mustard at all
vinegar	Lemon juice Lime juice
olive oil	**For a neutral taste** (lets other ingredients pop): Grapeseed oil Sunflower oil Avocado oil **For a stronger taste:** Walnut oil Hazelnut oil
nothing! (Prepare the recipe as is, or make one of the substitutions listed here, then add one or two of the tasty seasonings before you shake it.)	Grated garlic Chopped fresh herbs Minced anchovies (personal fave!) Chopped shallot or onion A small squirt of honey Grated lemon zest A drizzle of soy sauce A drizzle of fish sauce

The Essential Green Salad

New cooks often ask me what dish they should master first, and my answer is always "Learn to make the thing you love most." For my daughter, Dahlia, that means salad—she had this one nailed before she could even ride a bike. We love citrus juice as the acid in this dressing because it's brighter and milder than vinegar, and it tastes great along with the touch of garlic. For a stronger-flavored dressing, substitute the Mustard Vinaigrette on page 146.

1 to 2 tablespoons fresh **lemon juice** or lime juice

Fine sea salt

1 **garlic clove**, finely grated (optional; see Garlic Prep, page 13)

2 quarts **salad greens,** any kind you like

¼ cup **extra-virgin olive oil**, or more as needed

hands make the best salad tossers

The best salad tossers are clean hands. Hands are gentle and easy to control, won't smash delicate ingredients, and allow you to coat each component with dressing. But if you don't feel like getting your hands oily, use utensils made of wood or plastic, which are more gentle on the leaves than metal.

get it set

Set out all your ingredients.

1. Put the citrus juice and a pinch of salt in a salad bowl, and add the garlic, if using. Let the mixture sit for 5 minutes to dissolve the salt and mellow the garlic.

2. Add the salad greens and toss gently, preferably with your hands. Taste a leaf. If it's well balanced between salt and acid, drizzle in the oil and gently toss again. Otherwise, add a little more salt or a little more citrus juice to get the balance right; then add the oil, a drizzle at a time, tossing gently. Stop adding oil when the leaves feel lightly coated. Go easy. You can always add more later. Serve at once.

tips & tweaks

● Mixing the lemon juice and salt together before adding the oil gives the salt a chance to start dissolving, making for a more evenly seasoned salad. It's a slight but noticeable difference.

Classic Caesar Salad

with Unclassic Cheesy Croutons

Who doesn't love a Caesar? This is the classic salad; with plenty of garlic, lots of Parmesan cheese, and the traditional (optional) anchovy in creamy, pungent dressing. The special twist is that I add grated Parmesan to the croutons while they toast. The cheese attaches to the bread, melting and browning and making a crispy crust. The croutons are so good, you might want to double the crouton recipe and save some for noshing.

croutons

3 cups ½-inch cubes of **crusty bread** or baguette, preferably day-old (or older!)

1 to 2 tablespoons **extra-virgin olive oil**, for brushing

2 **garlic cloves,** smashed (see Garlic Prep, page 13)

2 tablespoons/ 13 grams **grated Parmesan cheese**

Kosher salt

caesar dressing

3 tablespoons **fresh lemon juice,** plus more to taste

6 tablespoons **extra-virgin olive oil**

2 tablespoons/ 13 grams **grated Parmesan cheese**

1 or 2 **oil-packed anchovy fillets** (optional)

1 **garlic clove** (see Garlic Prep, page 13)

1 teaspoon **Worcestershire sauce**

Kosher salt and **freshly ground black pepper**

salad

1 large or 2 small heads of **romaine lettuce,** separated into leaves, washed, and dried (see How to Wash & Dry Salad Greens, page 150)

3 tablespoons/ 20 grams **shredded Parmesan cheese**

Freshly ground black pepper

get it set

Put a plate next to the stove for the croutons.

Set out all your ingredients.

1. Make the croutons: Heat a large skillet over medium-low heat, then add the bread cubes. Toast them, stirring and tossing, until they start to dry out. If you are starting with dry, stale bread, this will only take about 2 minutes. For fresh bread, it might take more like 5 to 7 minutes. You'll know when the bread is hard when you poke it with a spatula or spoon.

2. When the bread is dry, add the oil and garlic and sauté until the bread and garlic turn golden brown all over, 3 to 5 minutes. Keep an eye on it. If the garlic starts to burn in spots, reduce the heat.

3. Sprinkle the cheese evenly all over the croutons and let it cook until it turns golden, 1 to 2 minutes. Use a slotted spoon to transfer the croutons to the plate, sprinkle lightly with salt, and let them cool. You can discard the garlic or, when it cools down,

(recipe continues)

chop it up and add it to the salad. It's mellow and sweet at this point, with only a little sharpness left after browning.

4. Make the Caesar dressing: In a blender or mini food processor, combine the lemon juice, olive oil, cheese, the anchovy fillets if using, and the garlic and Worcestershire. Blend until smooth, then taste and season with salt and pepper as needed, and with more lemon juice if you want it to be brighter. (You can also whisk everything together in a bowl; it won't have the same creaminess, but the flavors will still be great.)

5. Put the salad together: In a large salad bowl, toss the lettuce with dressing to coat (you may not need all of it). Sprinkle salad with the Parmesan and black pepper. Divide salad among four bowls and serve with the croutons on top.

tips & tweaks

● Many Caesar salad recipes call for egg yolks, but having made about a million Caesars, I find the dressing is lighter, brighter, and more pungent without them. But try it for yourself: In Step 4, add a raw egg yolk to the dressing, blending it in with the other ingredients (see How to Separate Eggs, page 37).

● Turn this salad into more of a meal. Add one of these to the salad bowl after tossing: • **Cooked chicken** • **Cooked salmon** • **A couple of jammy eggs** (see Egg Academy, page 30)

how to wash & dry salad greens

If you're buying fresh greens (which I recommend) instead of boxed prewashed greens, you'll need to wash them.

Pro tip: The best time to wash salad greens is right when you bring your greens home from the market.

1. Tear or cut the salad leaves into bite-size pieces.

2. Fill either a salad spinner bowl, a large mixing bowl, or a clean empty sink with cold water.

3. Add the greens and gently swish them around to shake off any dirt and sand. For very gritty or sandy greens, you might have to repeat this process as many as four or five times (spinach, I'm looking at you), using fresh water for each round. Taste a leaf to make sure all the grit is gone.

4. Scoop out the clean salad greens, using your hands, to keep all the sand and soil undisturbed at the bottom.

5. Take them for a spin in the salad spinner to dry. Or if you don't have a spinner, roll the greens loosely in a clean kitchen towel (you might need more than one towel if the first one gets too wet).

6. Place the washed greens in a resealable plastic bag with a slightly damp paper towel, or still wrapped in the kitchen towel, and refrigerate for up to a week.

Cute Baby Kale and Avocado Salad

Baby kale is more tender than regular old kale, and perfect for salads. To make the dressing the best it can be, use two or three different herbs—it makes the whole salad lighter and more flavorful. The avocado and the silky dressing add a lush creaminess to this hearty bowl.

buttermilk ranch dressing

½ cup **buttermilk** (or plain yogurt)

½ cup **mayonnaise**

1 fat **garlic clove**

3 tablespoons chopped **fresh chives** or scallion greens

3 tablespoons **mixed soft fresh herb leaves,** such as dill, mint, parsley, basil, and/or cilantro, in any combination

Salt and **freshly ground black pepper**

Squeeze of **fresh lemon juice** (optional)

salad

1 **avocado**

Squeeze of **fresh lemon juice**

Salt as needed

5 ounces / 5 cups **baby kale,** washed and dried (see How to Wash & Dry Salad Greens, page 150)

get it set

Set out all your ingredients.

1. Make the Buttermilk Ranch Dressing: In a blender or mini food processor, combine the buttermilk, mayo, garlic clove, chives, herbs, and a pinch each of salt and pepper. Blend or process until the mixture is smooth and light green in color, 1 to 2 minutes. Taste, and add more salt and pepper if needed, plus a squeeze of lemon juice if you want it to taste brighter.

2. Put the salad together: Using a paring knife, halve the avocado, twisting the halves to open it. Carefully remove the pit, then use a large spoon to scoop the avocado flesh out of the skin and onto a cutting board. Cut the avocado into ½-inch cubes. Squeeze a little lemon juice over them and sprinkle them with salt.

3. Put the kale in a salad bowl and toss it with some of the dressing, until the leaves are lightly coated. You may not need all of the dressing, and the remainder will keep in the fridge for up to 1 week (see Tips & Tweaks).

4. Add the avocado cubes to the bowl and very gently toss them with the kale, taking care not to smush them (see Hands Make the Best Salad Tossers, page 148). Serve the salad at once, before the kale wilts.

tips & tweaks

- Leftover ranch dressing is fantastic as a dip for all kind of veggies, especially carrots, radishes, and celery.

- Sprinkling the avocado with lemon and salt before it goes into the salad bowl helps season it thoroughly, without your having to toss it very much. This gives it oomph and keeps it from turning into mush.

- Feel free to switch up the greens:
  - **Arugula** (spicier)
  - **Romaine** (juicier)
  - **Baby spinach** (more delicate)
  - **Mixed baby greens** (more colorful)

- This salad is also great with the classic Caesar dressing on page 149.

Food Parties for Fun Food Fans

There's no such thing as a party without food. While some parties try to squeak by on chips and dips, better ones go to the next level by making food a main event. The best parties, though, are the ones where everyone makes the food together. These are food parties, and that's my jam.

You don't need a special occasion. All you need is people you like to hang out with. Set out the fixings for classic party dishes—like tacos, pizzas, burgers, hot dogs, or ice cream sundaes—and your guests will have a blast customizing their own meals. You don't have to worry if your cousin is still vegan, or if your BFF likes a shocking amount of onions, because at a food party, you do you.

Feel free to multiply or divide the amounts for any of these recipes to feed larger or smaller groups—and make what you can ahead of time. Then on the day, you'll be chill and totally prepared, and everyone will have a great time with all the options.

BFF Party: Burgers & Hot Dogs

Burgers and hot dogs are BFFs (pretty sure that stands for Burgers and FrankFurters), so of course they show up at parties together. They can share almost the same squad of toppings (except sauerkraut–that's all Hot Dog).

the plan
→

1 to 2 days before, or on the day:
make **Caramelized Onion Topping**, page 158

↓

1 day before or on the day:
make **Spicy Coleslaw Topping**, page 159

↓

On the day:
set out **Toppings**, page 161

↓

At the party:
cook burgers and hot dogs (see page 160)

caramelized onion topping

2 tablespoons **extra-virgin olive oil**

2 tablespoons **unsalted butter**

3 pounds **onions**, thinly sliced (see Onion Prep, page 12)

½ teaspoon **sugar**

¼ teaspoon **kosher salt**, plus more to taste

2 sprigs of **fresh rosemary, thyme, or other woody herb**

get it set

Set out all your ingredients.

1. Put a large heavy-bottomed pot or Dutch oven over medium-high heat. When it's hot, add the oil and butter and heat until the butter melts.

2. Add the onions, sugar, salt, and herbs to the pot, stirring to coat everything with the oil and butter. Let the onions cook, stirring them every once in a while, until they are golden and caramelized, 25 to 40 minutes. You'll need to stir more often towards the end of the cooking time so the onions don't burn. Keep an eye on the onions as they cook; if they start to look too brown (anything darker than golden), reduce the heat. And if they start to stick, add a tablespoon or two of water to the pot.

3. When the onions are soft and lightly browned all over, taste them and add more salt if needed. Let them cool, then remove the herb sprigs. You can use these immediately or store them in the refrigerator for up to 1 week.

spicy coleslaw topping

1 fat **garlic clove,** finely grated (see Garlic Prep, page 13)

2 teaspoons **cider vinegar** or fresh lemon juice, plus more to taste

½ teaspoon **kosher salt,** plus more to taste

Freshly ground black pepper

Hot sauce, such as Sriracha or Tabasco, to taste

½ cup **mayonnaise**

2 tablespoons **extra-virgin olive oil**

6 cups shredded **cabbage** (about ½ head, or use coleslaw mix)

2 medium **carrots,** peeled and grated (1 cup)

¼ cup chopped **fresh dill, parsley,** and/or another soft herb

get it set

Set out all your ingredients.

1. Put the garlic in a large bowl and add the vinegar, salt, a little black pepper, and a few dashes of hot sauce. Let it all sit for 5 minutes. The acid will mellow the garlic's pungency and help dissolve the salt.

2. Add the mayonnaise and olive oil, and whisk until smooth. Then add the cabbage, carrots, and herbs and toss well. Taste, and add more salt and vinegar if the coleslaw tastes flat. Coleslaw can be made up to 6 hours ahead and stored in the refrigerator.

How to Cook Burgers and Hot Dogs for a Crowd

Cooking burgers in a skillet works great for a small family dinner, but if you're making burgers or hot dogs for a hungry crowd, you'll save yourself a lot of work by using a broiler.

burgers

You'll need about ¼ pound of ground beef (or pork, lamb, turkey, chicken, or vegan meat) per burger. Form the meat into patties, using a light touch. Don't squeeze it–the meat should stay loosely packed so it doesn't get tough when it's cooked. The burgers can be formed and kept covered with plastic wrap in the fridge for up to 6 hours.

When you are ready to cook the burgers, place a rack 4 inches below the broiler element and heat the broiler to high. Put the patties on a lightly oiled, rimmed sheet pan, leaving space between them so they can get browned all over. Sprinkle them lightly with salt.

Broil until the burgers are nicely browned on top, 2 to 3 minutes. Then flip them and brown on the other side, another 2 to 3 minutes for medium-rare.

For cheeseburgers, add 1 slice of cheese (American, cheddar, Swiss, Gouda, mozzarella) to each burger patty after cooking, then return the pan to the broiler for another 15 to 30 seconds to melt the cheese.

hot dogs

Place 1 to 2 hot dogs (beef, chicken, turkey, pork, or vegan) per person on a rimmed sheet pan, leaving about an inch between them. Arrange the rack 4 inches below the broiler element, and heat the broiler to high. Broil the hot dogs until they brown and blister, 2 to 4 minutes. You don't have to flip them. Serve hot.

toppings

- **Ketchup**

- **Mustard**

- **Mayonnaise**

- **Sliced pickles**

- **Sliced raw onions** (see Onion Prep, page 12)

- **Quick Pickled Onions** (see Vegetarian Skillet Beans recipe, page 192)

- **Pickle relish**

- **Sauerkraut**

- **Kimchi**

- **Lettuce leaves:** 2 to 3 leaves per person; something soft like butter lettuce or red leaf is ideal

- **Sliced tomatoes:** about ¼ to ½ tomato per person, sprinkled with salt just before serving

- **Sliced avocado:** about ¼ avocado per person, sprinkled with salt just before serving

- **Sliced fresh or pickled jalapeños** (store-bought or see page 48)

- **Vegetarian Skillet Beans** (page 192) or **Your Own Secret Chili** (page 191) for chili dogs

- **Cooked bacon** (see page 41): crumble it up for the hot dogs; for burgers, cut the strips in half

- And don't forget the **buns**

Wrap Artists: Taco Party

Who doesn't love a taco? Crispy chunks of pork carnitas or velvety, spicy beans, wrapped in warm tortillas with a garnish of tangy salsa, crunchy shredded lettuce or cabbage, and plenty of sour cream or guac. You can make the filling or fillings up to two days ahead.

the plan
→

1 to 2 days before
make your filling(s):
Crispy Pork Carnitas, page 164
Barbecue-Sauced Chicken, page 165
Spicy Citrus Shrimp, page 166
Vegetarian Skillet Beans, page 192, and/or **Picadillo**, page 197

↓

On the day:
prep your **Taco Toppings**, page 167

↓

Just before the party:
warm your tortillas and set up your **Taco Assembly Line**, page 167

crispy pork carnitas

6 **garlic cloves**, finely grated (see Garlic Prep, page 13)

2½ teaspoons **kosher salt**

1 teaspoon **freshly ground black pepper**

2 teaspoons **ground cumin**

2 teaspoons **olive oil**, plus more for drizzling

2 teaspoons **fresh lime juice**

3 pounds **boneless pork butt** (also called pork shoulder)

½ cup **fresh orange juice** (from 2 to 3 oranges)

3 to 5 **fresh oregano sprigs** or 1 teaspoon dried oregano

1 **bay leaf**

get it set

Heat the oven to 325°F.

Set out all your ingredients.

1. In a small bowl, combine the garlic, salt, pepper, cumin, oil, and lime juice, stirring to make a paste.

2. Using a chef's knife, cut the pork into 3-inch chunks. Put them in a Dutch oven or other heavy pot. Rub the garlic paste all over the pork. Pour the orange juice and ¼ cup water over the pork, add the oregano and bay leaf, and cover the pot.

3. Bake for 2 hours. Then uncover the pot and use a fork to test the meat. If the fork goes in without much resistance and the pork feels soft, it's done. If not, re-cover the pot and bake for another 20 minutes, then test it again.

4. When the meat is soft (you should be able to easily stab through it with a fork), remove the pot from the oven and let the pork cool until it's just warm, about 1 hour at room temperature.

5. Using two forks or your fingers, shred the pork into bite-size pieces. Discard the bay leaf and oregano sprigs. At this point, you can let the meat cool completely, then store it, along with all of the accumulated juices, in the fridge for up to 5 days. Or it can sit out for up to 2 hours before you continue with the recipe.

6. To crisp up the pork for serving, heat the oven to 500°F. Spread the shredded pork and all the juices in an even layer on a rimmed sheet pan. Drizzle everything with a little oil. Roast the pork for 20 to 30 minutes, until most of the juices have cooked off and the meat is crispy. Keep an eye on the meat and toss it occasionally so the portion near the sides of the pan doesn't burn. Serve hot or warm.

barbecue-sauced chicken

1½ pounds **boneless, skinless chicken thighs**

Kosher salt, as needed

Extra-virgin olive oil, for drizzling

¾ cup **ketchup**

2 tablespoons **dark brown sugar**

2 tablespoons **cider vinegar**

1 tablespoon **Worcestershire sauce**

½ teaspoon **paprika**

1 **garlic clove**, finely grated or minced

¼ teaspoon **freshly ground black pepper**

get it set

Heat the oven to 400°F.

Set out all your ingredients.

1. Place the chicken thighs on a sheet pan. Season the chicken lightly with salt, then drizzle it with a little oil. Roast until the chicken is browned on top and cooked through, 25 to 30 minutes, depending on the size of the thighs (see Chicken: Is It Done Yet?, page 110). Remove the pan from the oven and let the chicken cool until you can handle it.

2. While the chicken is roasting, make the barbecue sauce: In a medium pot, stir together the ketchup, brown sugar, vinegar, Worcestershire, paprika, garlic, and pepper. Bring the mixture to a boil, then reduce it to a simmer. Let the sauce simmer until it has thickened and darkened in color, 10 to 15 minutes.

3. When the chicken is cool enough to handle, you can either shred it with your fingers or put it on a cutting board and chop it up with a chef's knife. Add the chicken to the sauce in the pot. Stir them together, reheating the mixture over low heat if it's cold. Then serve the chicken hot or warm.

tips & tweaks

● On its own, the sauce can be used anywhere you'd traditionally use a barbecue sauce: tossed with pulled pork, slathered on a burger, or drizzled over nachos. (To toss it with the pulled pork on the opposite page, you need twice as much, so you would double the sauce recipe.)

● This chicken is also delicious on its own or over rice, if you're not in the mood for tacos.

spicy citrus shrimp

1½ pounds peeled large **shrimp,** thawed if frozen

½ teaspoon **kosher salt**

2 tablespoons **unsalted butter,** divided

1 tablespoon **extra-virgin olive oil**

1 **garlic clove,** minced (see Garlic Prep, page 13)

½ teaspoon **chile powder**

¼ cup **fresh orange juice** (from 1 to 2 oranges)

1 tablespoon chopped **fresh cilantro, basil,** or other soft herb

get it set

Put a plate next to the stove for the shrimp. Set out all your ingredients.

1. Put the shrimp in a large bowl and toss them with the salt.

2. Heat a large (preferably nonstick) skillet over medium-high heat. When it's hot, add 1 tablespoon of the butter and the oil and let it heat until the butter melts. Add half of the shrimp in one layer, making sure not to crowd the pan. Cook for 1 to 2 minutes per side, until they turn pink and opaque, and transfer them to a plate. Repeat with the remaining shrimp. Set the shrimp aside.

3. Reduce the heat under the pan to medium, then add the remaining 1 tablespoon butter and let it melt. Stir in the garlic and chile powder. Cook until you can smell the garlic, about 1 minute.

4. Stir in the orange juice and cook until the sauce reduces slightly, about 1 minute. Return the shrimp to the pan, add the cilantro, and toss to coat. Transfer the shrimp to a serving bowl and serve immediately.

taco toppings

Leave room for toppings! However great your filling is–and your filling is definitely great–toppings add brightness, personality, and verve to a taco. Put out as many of these as you can and let everyone help themselves. For each topping, you need roughly 2 tablespoons to ½ cup per person.

- **Romaine lettuce, sliced**
- **Diced tomatoes**
- **Sliced avocados** (see page 161)
- **Shredded cabbage**
- **Sliced raw onions** (see Onion Prep, page 12) or scallions
- **Sliced radishes**
- **Lime wedges**
- **Cilantro sprigs**
- **Veggie Quick Pickles** (page 67)
- **Pickled jalapeños** (store-bought or see Chip-Crisp Quesadillas recipe, page 48)
- **Sliced raw jalapeños**
- **Salsa** (store-bought or homemade, see Chunky Cherry Tomato Salsa, page 61)
- **Guacamole** (store-bought or see The. Last. Guacamole. Recipe. Ever., page 63)
- **Sour cream**
- **Hot sauce**
- **Shredded cheddar or Mexican blend cheese**
- **Crumbled Cotija cheese**
- **Soft corn or flour tortillas, warmed** (see Tortilla Tips at right)

taco assembly line

Just before the party, set out your taco fillings and toppings in bowls with forks, spoons, or tongs to create a taco assembly line. Warm the tortillas and fillings if necessary. Tortillas and fillings go at the start of the line, then the toppings. Leave some elbow room between ingredients if you can.

tortilla tips

Corn tortillas are sturdy and flour tortillas are soft, but the main thing is to find high-quality fresh tortillas.

Tortillas should always be warmed and nestled in a clean dish cloth or towel to keep them that way throughout the meal. They release steam as they sit, which helps keep them supple and soft and ready for wrapping.

Here are three ways to keep them warm and ready until it's filling time:

Microwave: Stack a few tortillas on a microwave-safe plate, cover them with a damp paper towel, and pop them in the microwave for 30 seconds. Keep microwaving in 15-second bursts until they're warm and soft.

Oven: Wrap about 5 tortillas together in foil. Bake in a 350°F oven until heated through, 10 to 15 minutes.

Stovetop: Place 1 or 2 tortillas at a time in a heavy skillet set over medium-high heat and warm them until you see steam forming, about 30 seconds. Flip them over and heat for another 30 seconds or so, until heated through.

the plan →

Top This!
Pizza Party

Homemade pizza is better than any pizza you can buy. Sauce made from the best ingredients, a crust that's crisp and lightly chewy, fresh toppings, and everything put together just the way you like it—just try to beat that from a soggy cardboard box. At this party, everybody has fun together making their favorite individual pizzas, exactly the way they want them.

1 to 2 days before (earlier is better):

make **Classic Neapolitan Pizza Dough,** page 170

↓

1 day before or on the day:

make **Essential Pizza Sauce,** page 172

↓

On the day:

set up your **Toppings Station (including Pizza Garnishes),** page 173

↓

At the party:

Pizza Time! page 175

classic neapolitan pizza dough

Crispy-chewy crust with a deep, yeasty flavor, studded with giant air bubbles that turn black in the oven: this is the classic pie they make in Naples, where pizza was either invented or refined (experts can argue that one for days). If you're short on time and want to use store-bought pizza dough, you can. Most commercial doughs are large enough for 12-inch pies, so just halve them to make the individual pizzas. Note: you'll need to start this dough 24 to 48 hours before baking.

(See Weigh It Up, page 13.)

1½ teaspoons / 5 grams **active dry yeast** or instant yeast

1¾ cups / 400 mL / 396 grams warm (not hot) **water**

2 teaspoons **extra-virgin olive oil,** plus more for drizzling

4½ to 5 cups / 563 to 625 grams **all-purpose flour,** plus more for the work surface

2 teaspoons / 12 grams **kosher salt**

get it set

SPECIAL EQUIPMENT: Electric stand mixer fitted with the dough hook attachment, or a food processor (or use a large bowl and a wooden spoon)

Oil a large bowl for the dough.

Set out all your ingredients.

1. Combine the yeast, water, and oil in the bowl of an electric mixer or other large bowl, or in a food processor, and let sit until the yeast is foamy, about 5 minutes.

2. Using the dough hook or the food processor blade, beat or pulse in 4½ cups / 563 grams of the flour and the salt and mix until a smooth, slightly elastic dough forms,

2 to 3 minutes, gradually adding more flour, up to another ½ cup / 63 grams, as needed. Or use a wooden spoon to mix in the flour, switching to your hands if the dough gets too thick to mix with a spoon. Then knead the dough by hand: Flour a clean work surface, dump the dough onto it, and knead it energetically, leaning your weight into it. Stretch it out, then fold it back on itself. Give it a quarter turn and do it again, repeating until the dough is smooth and elastic, 5 to 7 minutes. (For more about yeasted doughs, see page 217.)

3. Place the dough in the oiled bowl and turn it so it's coated all over. Cover the bowl with a plate, a pot lid, or plastic wrap, and refrigerate it for at least 24 hours and up to 48 hours (the longer the better, but not more than 48 hours).

4. Divide the dough into 8 equal pieces. Shape each piece into a tight, compact ball. Put the dough balls on a sheet pan. Cover the pan well with plastic wrap and return it to the refrigerator to rest for at least 2 hours and up to 24 hours. (To bake the pizzas, see Pizza Time!, page 175.)

tips & tweaks

● To make whole-wheat pizza dough, substitute 1 cup / 120 grams whole-wheat flour for an equal amount of all-purpose flour. This makes the crust earthier, and it adds a bit of chewiness too.

● To make larger pizzas, form the dough into 4 balls instead of 8. (The larger pies might need an extra 5 to 10 minutes in the oven.)

essential pizza sauce

Tomato sauce for a pizza cooks right on the crust while the dough bakes in the oven. Cooking it only once preserves its fresh and vibrant flavor. Premade or store-bought marinara sauces are condensed and sweeter, without the bright tang of freshly made sauce. You *could* use that—but since it takes only a few minutes to whirl this together, I'd say homemade wins again!

1 (28-ounce) can **whole peeled tomatoes** (don't substitute fresh tomatoes here)

1 tablespoon **extra-virgin olive oil**

Kosher salt and **freshly ground black pepper,** as needed

1 **garlic clove,** finely grated (optional; see Garlic Prep, page 13)

1 or 2 **oil-packed anchovy fillets** (optional, for added umami depth of flavor)

¼ teaspoon dried **oregano** or 4 fresh **basil leaves** (optional)

get it set

Set out all your ingredients.

1. Put the tomatoes and all their liquid in a blender or food processor. Add the olive oil, a big pinch each of salt and pepper, and the optional garlic, anchovies, and oregano. Blend or process until the mixture is smooth-ish. Some lumps are fine.

2. Taste the sauce and add more salt and pepper if it seems flat. You may not need more, though, because pizza sauce shouldn't be highly seasoned. That's where the toppings come in.

tips & tweaks

● This recipe makes a lot of sauce, probably more than you'll need, so plan on freezing the extra to use the next time a pizza craving hits. Pizza sauce will keep for at least 5 days in the refrigerator, and you can freeze it for up to 1 year.

toppings station

Choose your own combinations of toppings, or try one from my list of favorites on page 172. These go on the pie just before baking. The key is not to overdo the toppings, or the crust can get soggy.

- **Sliced or grated mozzarella** (fresh mozzarella is best sliced, but if you're using packaged mozzarella, it should be shredded), about 2 ounces per person

- **Grated Parmesan or other cheeses** (Gruyère is nice with mushrooms; Monterey Jack is great with sliced jalapeños), ½ to 2 ounces per person

- **Fresh ricotta cheese,** about 2 ounces per person

- **Crumbled blue cheese or feta,** about 1 ounce per person

- **Sliced pepperoni or salami,** about 1 ounce per person

- **Anchovy fillets** (Personal favorite! Buy them oil-packed, in jars or cans, and place 2 to 4 per person out on a plate for easy access)

- **Olives,** sliced, about 2 tablespoons per person

- **Capers,** about 1 tablespoon per person

- **Cooked vegetables,** sliced or diced: broccoli, broccoli rabe, cauliflower, potatoes, sweet potatoes, brussels sprouts, asparagus, mushrooms, spinach, about ¼ cup per person

- **Raw vegetables and fruit,** thinly sliced or finely diced: garlic, onions, scallions, jalapeños or other fresh chiles, fennel, shaved butternut squash, cherry tomatoes, pineapple, grapes, lemons

- **Cooked meatballs** (small ones work best, about 1 inch in diameter; see Unmistakably Herby Meatballs, page 123)

- **Chopped roasted red peppers**

- **Chopped marinated artichoke hearts**

pizza garnishes

These garnishes, added to the pies after they come out of the oven, bring a pop of flavor. Use them in any combination you like, or skip them entirely.

- **Dried oregano**

- **Crushed red pepper flakes**

- **Garlic powder**

- **Grated Parmesan cheese**

- **Hot sauce, like Sriracha or Tabasco** (if you like these on grilled cheese, you'll love them on pizza!)

- **Baby arugula, salad greens, or spinach** (toss them with a little olive oil and lemon juice first)

some excellent combinations

↓

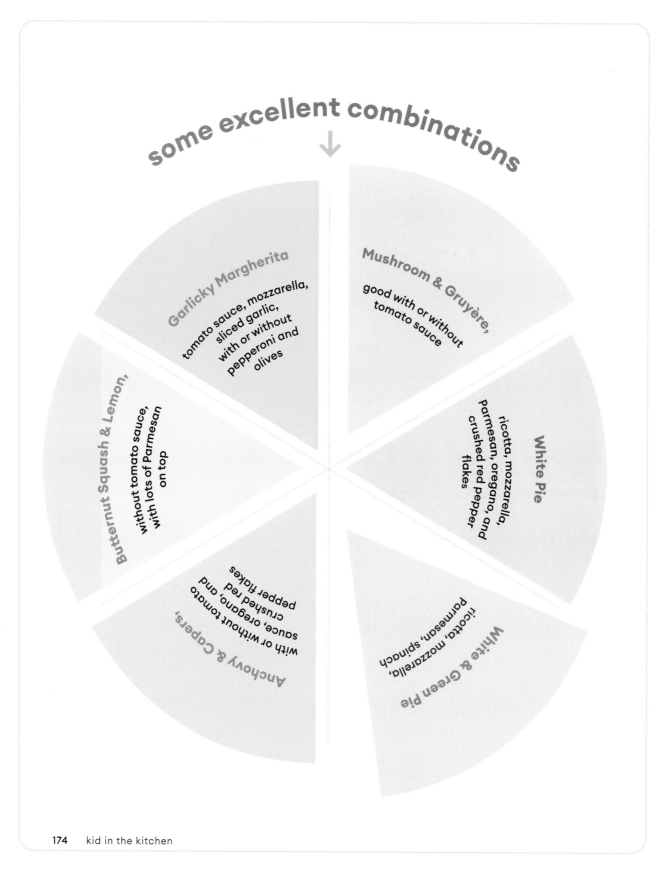

Garlicky Margherita
tomato sauce, mozzarella, sliced garlic, with or without pepperoni and olives

Mushroom & Gruyère,
good with or without tomato sauce

White Pie
ricotta, mozzarella, parmesan, oregano, and crushed red pepper flakes

White & Green Pie
ricotta, mozzarella, parmesan, spinach

Anchovy & Capers,
with or without tomato sauce, oregano, and crushed red pepper flakes

Butternut Squash & Lemon,
without tomato sauce, with lots of Parmesan on top

pizza time!

Once your dough has done its last chilling in the refrigerator, it's time to make the pizzas. Shape your dough, add the sauce and toppings, and bake 'em up.

Pizza Dough,
page 170

Essential Pizza Sauce, page 172

Toppings of choice, page 173

Extra-virgin olive oil, for drizzling

Flaky sea salt, such as Maldon, for sprinkling

Garnishes of choice, page 173

get it set

SPECIAL EQUIPMENT: Pizza stone or steel (optional); 1 sheet pan for each pizza

Set out all your ingredients.

1. Take the dough out of the fridge and let it sit at room temperature for 30 minutes. Meanwhile, place a pizza stone or steel, if using, on the middle rack in the oven. Heat the oven to 500°F. Allow the oven, and the baking stone or steel if using, to heat for 30 minutes.

2. Stretch and pull each dough ball into a 6-inch round (or sort of round, round-ish, or amoeba-shaped–it's all good). Put the dough onto sheet pans.

3. Top the pizzas as you like! Be sparing, though–you don't need a lot. Start with about 2 tablespoons of sauce per 6-inch pizza and 3 tablespoons for larger pizzas (unless you're skipping the sauce), and just a few tablespoons of toppings. Drizzle with a little olive oil and sprinkle with flaky salt.

4. Bake the pizzas. (If you are using a pizza stone or steel, bake one pan at a time directly on the stone or steel; otherwise put the pans on your oven racks.) Bake until the crusts are golden and the cheese, if using, is melted, 10 to 20 minutes. If you want the crust to be browned on top with singed air bubbles, you can then run the pizzas under the broiler for a minute or two (one sheet pan at a time), but this is optional.

5. Use a spatula to transfer the pizzas from the sheet pan to plates. Add any garnishes you like, and serve immediately.

tips & tweaks
- Leftover pizza dough freezes well. Wrap it in plastic wrap and put it in a resealable freezer bag. It will keep for up to 3 months. Thaw it overnight in the refrigerator, then pull it out of the fridge and let it warm up for 30 minutes before shaping.

- If you are making 12-inch pizzas, the pies may need an extra 5 to 10 minutes in the oven.

Any Day Ice Cream Sundae Party

the plan →

This party cuts right to point: dessert! This homemade vanilla bean ice cream isn't necessarily better than the fanciest stuff you can buy, but it is super easy (if you have an ice cream maker), fun to make, and extremely delicious. Plus, you get bragging rights. Homemade hot fudge sauce and butterscotch sauce, on the other hand, are way, way better than anything from a store. So if you've got the time, make it all yourself and reap the glory. If you're in a rush or don't have an ice cream maker, buy the ice cream, make the sauces.

1 to 5 days before (earlier is better):
make
Easy Vanilla Bean Ice Cream,
page 178

↓

1 day before:
make
Hot Fudge Sauce,
page 179
and/or
Butterscotch Sauce,
page 180

↓

On the day:
make
whipped cream,
page 181;
assemble the
Toppings Bar,
page 181

easy vanilla bean ice cream

(See Weigh It Up, page 13.)

1 **vanilla bean** or 1 teaspoon vanilla extract

2½ cups / 473 mL / 600 grams **heavy cream**

1½ cups / 355 mL / 368 grams **whole milk**

¾ cup / 150 grams **sugar**

2 tablespoons / 43 grams **honey** (or use agave syrup or corn syrup)

¼ teaspoon **kosher salt**

get it set

Put the bowl of your ice cream maker in the freezer 4 to 6 hours ahead, if necessary (check the directions).

Set out all your ingredients.

1. If you're using a vanilla bean, lay the bean on a cutting board and use a paring knife to split the bean in half lengthwise. Now, use the tip of the knife to scrape the black pulp and seeds out from the center of the bean. This is where the great, vanilla-y flavor is.

2. Put the scraped-out vanilla bean and the pulp into a medium saucepan. Add the cream, milk, sugar, and honey. Bring the mixture to a simmer, stirring to dissolve the honey. Turn off the heat and let the mixture cool completely. If you're using vanilla extract, stir it in now, after the ice cream base has cooled.

3. Cover the bowl and chill the ice cream base in the fridge for at least 6 hours or overnight (or up to 5 days).

4. Pull the vanilla bean out of the ice cream base (you can rinse it off, let it dry, and add it to your container of sugar to impart a vanilla flavor if you like). Churn the ice cream base in an ice cream maker according to the manufacturer's instructions. Transfer the ice cream to a container, cover, and freeze for at least 4 hours before serving.

5. Take the ice cream out of the freezer 20 to 30 minutes before serving; otherwise it might be too hard to scoop.

hot fudge sauce

(See Weigh It Up, page 13.)

¼ cup / 21 grams **unsweetened cocoa powder** (either natural or Dutch process; see Cocoa Two Ways, page 260)

⅔ cup / 158 mL / 160 grams **heavy cream**

½ cup / 100 grams **sugar**

¼ cup / 59 mL / 85 grams **honey, agave syrup, or light corn syrup**

⅛ teaspoon **kosher salt**

8 ounces / 227 grams **bittersweet chocolate,** chopped

4 tablespoons / ½ stick / 57 grams **unsalted butter**

1 tablespoon **vanilla extract**

get it set

Set out all your ingredients.

1. In a small saucepan set over medium-low heat, combine the cocoa powder with ⅓ cup of water and whisk well. Bring to a boil, whisking until smooth.

2. Add the cream, sugar, honey, and salt to the pot. Cook, stirring constantly, until the sugar dissolves, 2 to 3 minutes. Add the chocolate and the butter, whisking until the chocolate is melted and the mixture is smooth, about 1 minute longer.

3. Continue to whisk until the sauce is thickened and glossy, 4 to 6 minutes. Then whisk in the vanilla and remove from the heat.

4. Use the sauce immediately, or let it cool and then transfer it to an airtight container and refrigerate it for up to 1 week. Reheat the sauce in a pot on the stove over low heat, or in the microwave. If it gets cold during the party, pop it back in the microwave or on the stove for a minute or so to heat it up again. Hot fudge should be hot!

butterscotch sauce

(See Weigh It Up, page 13.)

8 tablespoons / 1 stick / 113 grams **unsalted butter**

1 cup / 237 mL / 240 grams **heavy cream**

1 cup / 200 grams **dark brown sugar**

½ teaspoon **vanilla extract**

½ teaspoon **kosher salt**

get it set

Set out all your ingredients.

1. Put the butter in a medium heavy-bottomed pot and place it over medium heat. Let the butter melt, then stir in the cream and brown sugar, making sure to mix well.

2. Bring the mixture to a boil, then reduce the heat and let it simmer for 5 minutes, stirring occasionally to make sure all the sugar has melted.

3. Remove the pot from the heat and stir in the vanilla and salt. Let the sauce cool completely before using, or store the cooled sauce in an airtight container in the refrigerator for up to 1 week. Let the cold sauce come to room temperature before using it, which can take up to 4 hours if your kitchen is on the cooler side. Or microwave the sauce for 30 seconds or so, give it a stir, and repeat until it no longer feels cold but isn't yet warm.

tips & tweaks

● This sauce is multipurpose: use it as an ice cream topping, as a pancake or waffle topper, or as a drizzle on your morning granola and yogurt. You can also add it as a thin layer (along with the frosting) between cake layers, or as an additional flavor in hot chocolate.

toppings bar

Put out the toppings in bowls with spoons, and lay out ice cream scoops, a sundae glass or bowl for each person, and plenty of napkins. Warm up the hot fudge sauce, and make the whipped cream. To keep the ice cream cold, you can put it in a bowl of ice, but this is optional.

- **Whipped cream** (right), **Hot Fudge Sauce** (page 179), and **Butterscotch Sauce** (page 180)

- **Chopped toasted nuts:** Almonds, hazelnuts, walnuts, pecans, or peanuts

- **Sliced bananas:** To give your sundae banana-split vibes

- **Sliced strawberries** or other berries, or other sliced fruit (mangos, pineapple, etc.)

- **Cookie crumble:** Crumble up your favorite cookies

- **Sprinkles:** Both chocolate and rainbow because more is more

- **Candy:** M&M's, Reese's Pieces or chopped peanut butter cups, crushed candy canes or peppermint candies, marshmallows, toffee bits

- **Shredded coconut:** Either sweetened or unsweetened

- **Chocolate chips:** Regular or mini; semisweet, bittersweet, butterscotch, peanut butter

- **Breakfast cereal:** Use anything from cornflakes to Rice Krispies to the sugariest cereal in the aisle.

- **Maraschino cherries:** Yes, these are kind of waxy, but they do look good in a photo.

how to whip cream

Start by putting 1½ cups cold heavy cream, for 6 to 8 servings (or double the ingredients for more), in a bowl that's larger than you might think you need. If you like, sweeten it to taste with 1 to 3 tablespoons confectioners' sugar (not all whipped cream is sweetened—it's up to you) and add a dash of vanilla extract (also optional). The easiest way to whip the cream is to use an electric mixer fitted with the whisk or beaters, which will whip it in 1 to 2 minutes on high speed. Stop whipping when the cream is thick and mounds nicely on a spoon; if you overwhip it, you'll end up with butter (yummy, but not what you were going for).

You can also use a whisk and some elbow grease: Start whipping, and when your arm gets tired, pass it to a friend until they're tired, and back to you. It's kind of fun and magical to watch the cream gradually inflate and thicken.

Whipped cream can be made up to 2 hours ahead of serving and kept cold in the fridge. But don't whip it up much before that or it may deflate.

One-Pot Meals

Get Rich Quick Chicken Stock

Chicken stock is the secret behind the richest, most flavorful soups, stews, and sauces, as well as a lot of other dishes. Homemade stock adds a layered complexity and (probably) superpowers to your dish. And since it's simple to make, it's obvious that homemade stock is the best way to go. Here are three ways to make it.

3 pounds meaty **chicken bones** (see Tips & Tweaks)

6 **garlic cloves**, peeled or unpeeled

5 to 7 **fresh thyme** or **dill sprigs**

5 to 7 **fresh parsley sprigs**

1 to 2 **celery stalks**

1 large **carrot**

1 large **onion**, halved but not peeled (see Onion Prep, page 12)

1 tablespoon **sea salt**, or to taste

1 **whole clove** or star anise pod

1 **bay leaf**

1 teaspoon **whole black peppercorns**

2 to 4 (¼-inch-thick) slices **fresh ginger**, peeled or unpeeled (optional; see Tips & Tweaks)

get it set

Set out all your ingredients.

in a stockpot

1. Put the bones in a large stockpot along with all the remaining ingredients. Add enough water to cover the ingredients by 2 inches.

2. Bring everything to a simmer over high heat, then reduce the heat to low and let the stock simmer gently for 2 to 2½ hours (just a few slow bubbles should break the surface).

in an electric pressure cooker

1. Put the bones in an electric pressure cooker along with all the remaining ingredients. Add enough water to barely cover the ingredients.

2. Cook on high pressure for 1 hour. Then either let the pressure release naturally or use the quick release (it doesn't matter which).

in a slow cooker

1. Put the bones in a slow cooker along with all the remaining ingredients. Add enough water to cover the ingredients by 1 inch.

2. Cook on low for 10 to 12 hours.

3. The stock is done when it tastes delicious. You might need to add a little more salt to bring out the flavor, but don't salt it too much. It should be gently seasoned. Let the stock cool for 2 to 4 hours, uncovered, before proceeding with the next steps.

4. Using tongs or a slotted spoon, remove the chicken pieces and the vegetables from the stock and discard them (all the flavor has moved from the meat to your stock, so there's no point in trying to make chicken salad out of that stuff).

5. Put a strainer or colander over (or in) a very large bowl. (If you want a very clear stock, you can line your colander with cheesecloth, but I usually skip it.) Pour the stock through it. If the stockpot is too heavy to lift, use a ladle to transfer the stock to the strainer or colander. When all the stock is strained, discard the solids left in the strainer.

6. Chicken stock can be refrigerated for up to 5 days or frozen for up to 6 months.

tips & tweaks

● You can often buy meaty chicken bones—bones with some meat still clinging to them, such as chicken backs—from a butcher or the butcher department at a supermarket.

● Save the carcass (or even just some bones) from a chicken you've roasted—it's perfect for stock. Simmer some fresh raw chicken along with the cooked bones to give the stock the deepest flavor. You'll need 3 pounds of bones altogether.

Cozy Day Chicken Noodle Soup

Nothing out-cozies chicken soup. And since we're talking a one-pot situation here, this soup, with chunks of chicken, carrots, and celery and flecks of green herbs, is the easiest soup ever. You can swap out the noodles for orzo, macaroni, or rice. Eat this soup to feel healthier or just to warm yourself from the inside out. The aroma alone will cure just about anything that's getting you down.

1 pound **boneless, skinless chicken parts** (thighs or breasts or a combination)

2 **carrots**, thinly sliced

2 **celery stalks**, sliced

1½ quarts **chicken stock**, homemade (see page 184) or store-bought

Kosher salt

1 **garlic clove**, finely grated (see Garlic Prep, page 13)

Cooked egg noodles, rice noodles, small pasta shapes like orzo or macaroni, or **rice**, for serving (see Tips & Tweaks)

Chopped **fresh dill** or **parsley**

get it set

Place a cutting board next to the stove for the cooked chicken.

Set out all your ingredients.

1. Put the chicken, carrots, and celery in a large pot and cover them with the stock. Bring to a simmer over high heat. Then reduce the heat and simmer until the chicken is cooked through, 20 to 30 minutes (dark meat takes longer than white meat). Stir in a big pinch of salt and the garlic.

2. Use tongs to remove the chicken from the pot and place it on the cutting board (leave the veggies in the stock).

3. Taste the stock and add more salt if needed. When the meat is cool enough to handle, chop or shred the chicken meat into bite-size pieces and return them to the pot.

4. Add the noodles, pasta, or rice and let them heat in the soup for a minute or two. Serve the soup topped with the fresh dill.

tips & tweaks

● Adding cooked rice or noodles to the soup just before serving keeps them from turning soggy and keeps the stock nice and clear (the starch from the noodles or rice can make it cloudy). But if you're in a hurry, you *can* cook them in the stock: After removing the chicken in Step 2, add ½ cup rice or 6 ounces noodles and let them simmer in the stock until tender (15 to 17 minutes for rice, 3 to 7 minutes for noodles, depending on the shape). Add the chicken to the soup and serve immediately.

Mexican Chicken Soup & Chips

If chips and salsa magically morphed into a warm soup, this is what you'd get. Make it more or less spicy by tweaking the amount of chipotle peppers you stir in. If you can't find chipotles (see Tips & Tweaks), substitute a tablespoon of chili powder. This is a great use of a rotisserie chicken or leftover cooked chicken.

2 tablespoons **extra-virgin olive oil**

1 cup diced **red onion** (see Onion Prep, page 12), plus more for serving (optional)

1 **poblano chile** or green bell pepper, seeded and diced

2 **garlic cloves,** finely chopped (see Garlic Prep, page 13)

1 teaspoon **ground cumin**

½ to 1 **chipotle in adobo,** seeded and minced (see Tips & Tweaks)

4 cups **chicken stock,** homemade (see page 184) or store-bought

1 (15-ounce) can **whole peeled tomatoes,** broken up with your fingers, juices reserved

2 cups shredded **cooked chicken,** homemade (from one of the chicken recipes on pages 106 to 113) or from a store-bought rotisserie chicken

1½ teaspoons **kosher salt,** plus more as needed

for serving

Lime wedges

Tortilla chips

Diced avocado (optional)

Fresh cilantro leaves (optional)

get it set

Set out all your ingredients.

1. Place a medium pot over medium-high heat, add the oil, and let it heat up for about 20 seconds. It will shimmer and thin out as it heats, but shouldn't get hot enough to start to smoke. Add the onion and chile and cook, stirring from time to time, until the vegetables are soft, 7 to 10 minutes. Then stir in the garlic, cumin, and chipotle; cook for 1 minute more, until you can smell the garlic. Keep an eye on it–garlic burns really quickly.

2. Add the stock, tomatoes with their juices, chicken, and salt. Simmer until the tomatoes are broken down, about 25 minutes. Squeeze in 1 or 2 wedges of lime to brighten things up (taste it to check if it's enough), and add more salt if needed.

3. To serve, ladle the soup into bowls and float a handful of tortilla chips on top. If you like, top with diced avocado, red onion, and cilantro. Serve with more lime wedges.

tips & tweaks

● Chipotles are jalapeños that have been dried and smoked. They're a little hotter than fresh jalapeños but not hot enough to burn your mouth. For this recipe, you want to get the kind that comes in a jar or can, packed with adobo sauce (not the dried kind). Make sure to take the seeds out, and wash your hands with soap after chopping them (see Chile Pepper Alert, page 193).

Leave out:	Add instead:
Chicken stock	Vegetable stock
Chicken	(choose one or more, adding up to 2 cups) • Cubed tofu • Roasted cauliflower and mushrooms • Canned chickpeas or white beans

make it vegetarian

tips & tweaks

● Chili tastes even better a day or two after you cook it, making it a five-star leftover. You can balance the heat by serving this with Crispy Skillet Cornbread (page 213) or tortilla chips.

● Garnishes like sliced scallions or onion, diced fresh tomato, or diced avocado are a great fresh contrast to the slow-simmering flavor of chili. A dollop of sour cream or yogurt adds both a different temperature and texture to the dish.

Your Own Secret Chili Recipe

Every cook has their closely guarded chili recipe, so isn't it time you started working on yours? Try this foolproof recipe a couple of times, and then you can experiment with your dream chili ingredients. Use a different bean or meat (vegan meat works great here), or add your own mix of chiles. Chili can be made a million different ways. Which one will be yours?

1 tablespoon **extra-virgin olive oil** or bacon grease

2 pounds **ground beef, dark meat turkey,** or **vegan meat**

Kosher salt, as needed

½ teaspoon **freshly ground black pepper,** plus more to taste

1½ tablespoons **tomato paste**

1 medium **red** or **green bell pepper,** seeded and diced

1 medium **onion,** finely chopped (see Onion Prep, page 12)

2 **garlic cloves,** minced (see Garlic Prep, page 13)

1 to 2 fresh **chile peppers** (such as jalapeño, serrano, or poblano), seeded and finely chopped (see Chile Pepper Alert, page 193), to taste

1 to 3 tablespoons **chili powder**

1 teaspoon **ground cumin**

1 (28-ounce) can **diced tomatoes** with their juices

2 (15-ounce) cans **kidney beans** or **black beans** (or use one of each), drained and rinsed

1 to 2 teaspoons **fresh lime juice**

Chopped **fresh cilantro** or **parsley,** for serving

Lime wedges, for serving

get it set

Place a plate next to the stove to hold the browned meat.

Set out all your ingredients.

1. Place a large heavy pot or Dutch oven over medium-high heat. Add the oil and let it heat up for about 20 seconds. It will thin out, but it shouldn't smoke (if it does, move the pan off the heat for a few seconds). Add the ground meat and cook, breaking it up with a spoon, until well browned, 5 to 7 minutes. Season with 1 teaspoon salt and the pepper. Transfer meat to the plate.

2. Add the tomato paste to the pot. Cook, stirring, until the paste is golden brown, 1 to 2 minutes. Stir in the bell pepper, onion, garlic, and chiles. Cook until the vegetables soften, 7 to 10 minutes. Stir in the chili powder, cumin, and a pinch of salt; cook for 1 minute. Return the meat to the pan and add the tomatoes and their juices, the beans, ½ cup of water, and ½ teaspoon salt. Reduce the heat to medium and simmer uncovered for 35 to 45 minutes, until thick. Taste the chili and season it with the lime juice and more salt if you like. Ladle the chili into bowls. Sprinkle with cilantro if using, and serve with lime wedges.

Vegetarian Skillet Beans
(with Quick Pickled Onions!)

SERVES 4 TO 6

This is basically a chili, but instead of meat the main attraction is velvety, saucy beans. It's hearty, spicy, bean-y, and quick to make. Serve it by itself, with cornbread (page 213), or in a taco (see page 163). The quick pickles give it zip.

for the pickled onions

1 **lime**, halved

½ small **red** or **white onion** or 1 large shallot, thinly sliced (see Onion Prep, page 12)

Pinch of **salt**

Pinch of **granulated sugar**

for the beans

2 tablespoons **olive oil**

1 large **onion**, chopped (see Onion Prep, page 12)

Kosher salt, as needed

2 **garlic cloves**, minced (see Garlic Prep, page 13)

1 **jalapeño**, seeded and minced (optional; see Chile Pepper Alert, page 193)

1 tablespoon **chili powder**, plus more to taste

1 teaspoon dried **oregano**, plus more to taste

2 (15-ounce) cans **kidney beans**, drained and rinsed

1 (15-ounce) can **diced tomatoes**, with their juices

optional garnishes

fresh cilantro, diced avocado, sour cream, store-bought or homemade **salsa** (see Chunky Cherry Tomato Salsa, page 61)

get it set

Set out all your ingredients.

1. First make the **pickled onions** so they can sit while you prepare the chili: Squeeze the lime juice into a small bowl, and add the onion, a large pinch of salt, and a small pinch of sugar. Stir and then let the mixture sit for 20 minutes while the chili cooks.

2. Cook the beans: Place a large ovenproof skillet over medium-high heat, then add the oil and let it heat up for about 20 seconds. It will shimmer and thin out as it heats, but it shouldn't get hot enough to start to smoke (if it does, move the pan off the heat immediately for a few seconds). Stir in the onion and a pinch of salt, and sauté until the onion softens and turns golden at the edges, about 5 minutes.

3. Add the garlic, jalapeño if using, chili powder, and oregano and sauté until you can smell the garlic, 1 to 2 minutes. Keep an eye on it–garlic burns really quickly. Add the drained beans, the tomatoes with their juices, and a few large pinches of salt. Simmer until the tomatoes break down, about 20 minutes.

4. Taste, and add more salt, chili powder, and/or oregano as needed. Serve with pickled onions and any of the garnishes you like. If there are leftovers, they'll keep getting better as they sit in the fridge (where they'll keep for up to 5 days).

chile pepper alert

Warning: Jalapeños and other hot chile peppers are no joke! They are very spicy and somewhat high maintenance: The seeds and the veins are where a lot of that peppery heat lives, so unless you're going for burn-your-mouth spicy, they need to be removed with a paring knife. Be careful not to touch your face or rub your eyes by accident when handling the peppers. Their oils, which stay on your fingers, can really burn. The best thing to do when handling chiles is to WEAR GLOVES. At the very least, wash your hands really well with soap and water after you're done.

tips & tweaks

● The pickled onions are a great garnish on so many dishes, so you might want to double the recipe and store the extra in the fridge for up to 2 weeks. Use them on sandwiches, with eggs, or on any of the grain bowls on pages 134 to 142.

Easy Skillet Chicken Parm

SERVES 4

With its garlicky, chunky tomato sauce and stretchy, gooey mozzarella topping, this chicken parm is a gorgeous cheese-topped classic. This version is lighter and a whole lot quicker than the traditional version, no deep-frying required. You can easily change it up to make vegetable parm—which is just as cheesy and good (see Tips & Tweaks, page 196).

1¼ pounds thin-sliced **chicken breast cutlets**

¾ teaspoon **kosher salt**

¾ teaspoon dried **oregano**

3 tablespoons **extra-virgin olive oil**, plus more as needed

1 **garlic clove,** minced (see Garlic Prep, page 13)

2 cups **marinara** or other tomato sauce, homemade (see Home-Base Spaghetti, page 90) or store-bought

4 tablespoons / 25 grams **grated Parmesan cheese,** divided

¼ teaspoon **freshly ground black pepper**

6 ounces **fresh mozzarella**, grated (1½ cups)

Chopped **fresh basil,** for garnish (optional)

get it set

Position an oven rack 4 inches below the broiler element, and turn on the broiler.

Place a large plate next to the stove to hold the cooked chicken pieces.

Set out all your ingredients.

1. Sprinkle the chicken cutlets all over with the salt and the oregano.

2. Place a large ovenproof skillet over medium-high heat, then add 2 tablespoons of the oil and let it heat up for about 20 seconds. It will shimmer and thin out as it heats, but it shouldn't get hot enough to start to smoke (if it does, move the pan off the heat for a few seconds). Add as many pieces of the seasoned chicken to the skillet as will fit in one layer without overlapping (usually 2 or 3 pieces; don't crowd the pan or the chicken will steam rather than brown). Let the chicken cook until it is pale golden on the bottom (about 2 minutes), then use tongs to flip it, and let it get golden on the

(recipe continues)

other side, another 1 to 2 minutes. Transfer the cooked chicken to the plate, and continue cooking the remaining chicken, adding more oil if the pan looks dry.

3. When all the chicken is browned, add the remaining 1 tablespoon of the oil to the pan (no need to clean the pan first) and stir in the garlic. Cook, stirring, for 30 seconds to 1 minute, just until you can smell it. Then stir in the marinara sauce, 2 tablespoons of the Parmesan, and the pepper, and let the sauce come to a simmer.

4. Nestle the chicken cutlets into the sauce, then spoon the sauce over to cover them (mostly covered–the chicken can poke through a bit).

5. Sprinkle the mozzarella and the remaining 2 tablespoons Parmesan evenly over the chicken. Transfer the skillet to the broiler and broil for 1 to 3 minutes, until the cheese has melted and browned in spots. Keep your eye on it–the cheese can go from melted to burnt in under a minute. Sprinkle with the basil if using, and serve immediately.

tips & tweaks

● To make this spicy, add a big pinch of crushed red pepper flakes to the pan along with the garlic in Step 3.

● To make a vegetarian version, skip the meat and substitute 6 cups cooked vegetables. Just add them to the pan with the sauce in Step 4. Some excellent options:

• Roasted winter squash
• Roasted or sautéed cauliflower and broccoli
• Sautéed greens
• Broiled or sautéed zucchini
• Roasted or sautéed eggplant
• Roasted or sautéed mushrooms
• Any combination of the above

Picadillo

Spicy Ground Meat with Raisins and Olives

Raisins and olives may sound like a funny combination at first, but in this traditional Latin American ground meat dish, the sweetness and saltiness blend into the meat as it cooks, making it rich and delicious. Picadillo is perfect as a taco filling (see page 163), and it's great spooned over rice (see page 242). Or try it topped with a fried egg, so the yolk can run all over the meat like a silky, creamy sauce.

2 tablespoons **extra-virgin olive oil**

1 small **onion**, diced (see Onion Prep, page 12)

½ red **bell pepper**, diced

4 **garlic cloves**, minced (see Garlic Prep, page 13)

2 teaspoons **ground cumin**

1 teaspoon dried **oregano**

1 pound **ground meat** (beef, pork, turkey, lamb, or chicken; vegan meat works here, too)

1 teaspoon **kosher salt**

½ teaspoon **freshly ground black pepper**

1 cup canned **diced tomatoes** with their juices

¼ cup **raisins**, either black or golden

½ cup **green olives**, pitted and sliced, or 1 tablespoon drained capers

get it set

Set out all your ingredients.

1. Place a large ovenproof skillet over medium-high heat, then add the oil and let it heat up for about 20 seconds. It will shimmer and thin out as it heats, but it shouldn't get hot enough to start to smoke (if it does, move the pan off the heat immediately for a few seconds). Stir in the onion and bell pepper, and cook until they start to soften, 4 to 6 minutes. Then stir in the garlic, cumin, and oregano, and cook until you can smell the garlic, 1 minute. Keep an eye on it—garlic burns really quickly.

2. Stir in the ground meat, salt, and pepper, and use a spoon to break up the meat into small chunks. Sauté until it's no longer pink, about 3 minutes, then push the meat into a single layer and cook, without stirring it, until it is browned, about 5 minutes.

3. Stir in the tomatoes with their juices, the raisins, and the olives. Bring to a simmer, then reduce the heat to medium-low, cover the pan, and cook, stirring occasionally, to let the flavors meld, about 10 minutes. Serve hot or warm.

tips & tweaks

● If you're not a raisin fan, just leave them out. Or substitute other dried fruit, like chopped dried apricots or cranberries, to add a sweet note.

Cheesy Skillet Black Beans

SERVES 6

Scientists have proven, of course, that all foods are better when topped with melted cheese. I find this is doubly true of beans. Serve this over rice (see page 242), with cornbread (see page 213), or with tortillas, for a meal that walks the line between a vegetarian chili and a cheesy, seven-layer bean dip, but might be better than either one.

2 tablespoons **extra-virgin olive oil**

2 **garlic cloves,** minced (see Garlic Prep, page 13)

1 teaspoon **ground cumin** or smoked paprika

1 cup **salsa,** homemade (see Chunky Cherry Tomato Salsa, page 61) or your favorite store-bought

2 (15-ounce) cans **black beans,** preferably not unsalted (see Tips & Tweaks), drained

1 cup chopped **fresh cilantro** or **parsley**

Salt, as needed

Hot sauce, to taste (optional)

2½ cups / 10 ounces shredded **Monterey Jack cheese** (pepper jack if you like some heat)

stirring, for about a minute or until you can smell it. Keep an eye on it–garlic burns really quickly. Then stir in the cumin and cook for 15 seconds longer, to toast it slightly and bring out the flavor.

2. Pour in the salsa and bring it to a simmer. Let it simmer for 5 minutes, then add the beans and continue to simmer for 5 minutes longer. Stir in the herbs. Taste, and season with salt as needed and with hot sauce if you want it spicy.

3. Sprinkle the cheese over the beans. Transfer the skillet to the broiler and broil for 1 to 3 minutes, until the cheese melts and bubbles (keep your eye on it–it can go from melted to burnt in less than a minute). Serve hot or warm.

get it set

Position an oven rack 4 inches below the broiler, and then turn on the broiler.

Set out all your ingredients.

1. Place a large ovenproof skillet over medium-high heat, then add the oil and let it heat up for about 20 seconds. It will shimmer and thin out as it heats, but it shouldn't get hot enough to start to smoke (if it does, move the pan off the heat for a few seconds). Stir in the garlic and cook,

tips & tweaks

● Canned beans that have been cooked with salt taste a lot better than unsalted beans. So look for salt in the ingredients list on the label, and avoid sodium-free beans if possible.

● You can use another good melting cheese in place of the Monterey Jack. Cheddar, Swiss, and mozzarella are all good substitutes.

Shrimp Scampi Skillet Dinner

Garlicky, buttery, and made in one pan. The sauce is the richest part of a shrimp scampi (almost better than the shrimp itself), so in this version it's also used to cook the orzo pasta, which soaks it up and becomes so super-infused with flavor that it's hard to stop eating it. Sprinkle some Parmesan on top for added oomph. Parm is not traditional for scampi, but it's yummy, and anyway the Scampi Police are not a thing.

1 **lemon**

1¼ pounds pelled large **shrimp** (thawed if frozen)

1 teaspoon chopped **fresh rosemary leaves** (optional but nice; see Tips & Tweaks, page 202)

½ teaspoon **kosher salt**, plus more to taste

Pinch of **crushed red pepper flakes** (optional)

4 tablespoons / ½ stick / 57 grams **unsalted butter**

2 tablespoons **extra-virgin olive oil**

4 **garlic cloves,** minced (see Garlic Prep, page 13)

2 cups **seafood, vegetable,** or **chicken stock,** homemade (see page 184 for chicken and vegetable) or store-bought

¾ cup **orzo**

2 tablespoons chopped **fresh parsley** or **basil**

Grated Parmesan cheese, for serving (optional)

get it set

Place a plate or bowl next to the stove to hold the sautéed shrimp.

Set out all your ingredients.

1. Using a Microplane or other fine grater, grate the zest from the lemon and put it in a large bowl. Add the shrimp, rosemary, salt, and red pepper flakes if using, and toss well.

2. In a large skillet, melt the butter with the olive oil over medium-high heat. Add the garlic and cook for 30 seconds to 1 minute, until you can smell it. Keep an eye on it–garlic burns really quickly. Add the shrimp mixture and sauté it for 2 minutes, until the shrimp turn bright pink but aren't quite cooked through.

3. Using a slotted spoon, transfer the shrimp to the plate or bowl.

(recipe continues)

4. Pour the stock into the skillet and bring it to a simmer. Add the orzo and reduce the heat to low. Cover the pan and let the orzo cook for 10 to 13 minutes, until it is not quite al dente (carefully taste one to see if it's ready, making sure to blow on it to cool it first). (The orzo will finish cooking in the next step.)

5. Uncover the skillet and add the shrimp to the orzo, stirring well. Cover and let the shrimp and orzo finish cooking together, 2 to 3 minutes.

6. Halve the lemon and squeeze the juice all over the orzo and shrimp. Add the chopped herbs and toss well. Taste, and add more salt if needed. Sprinkle with the Parmesan if you like. Serve hot.

umami, the fifth taste

There are five basic tastes that your taste buds can sense: sweet, salty, sour, bitter—and umami. Everybody knows the first four, but *umami* is a less familiar word. It means "deliciousness" in Japanese, and refers to a savory, funky, complex quality that makes some foods extra tasty: the rich flavor of Parmesan cheese, cooked tomatoes (especially ketchup and tomato paste), soy and fish sauce, anchovies, and the browned edges of a piece of buttered toast. Umami is a shorter way to say, "Wow, that tastes good in a way that's not just sweet, salty, bitter, or sour, but just deeply YUM." Which is good, because it would take too long to say that when you're happily eating.

tips & tweaks

● If you don't have fresh rosemary, just leave it out. Don't try to substitute dried rosemary here: The shrimp don't cook for long enough to soften the dried stuff, and the texture will be prickly.

● I love adding a couple of anchovies to the pan along with the garlic. Mince a fillet or two and throw them in the pan. They will melt into the sauce, leaving umami deliciousness in their wake.

Pajeon

Korean Scallion and Veggie Pancakes

Pancakes for dinner? Oh yeah! *Pajeon*—traditional Korean crispy pancakes filled with scallions and veggies—are officially dinner pancakes, though you can also make them for lunch or brunch. The kimchi adds a salty, tangy, spicy flavor to the pancakes, which makes them especially savory. And the sesame-soy dipping sauce is so good, you'll want to use it for other things. Try pouring it over rice or jammy eggs (see Egg Academy, page 30) at any meal.

for the dipping sauce

- ⅓ cup **soy sauce**
- 1½ tablespoons **rice vinegar**
- 2 teaspoons finely grated **fresh ginger** or **garlic**, or both (optional; see Garlic Prep, page 13, and How to Prep Ginger, page 86)
- 1 teaspoon **toasted (Asian) sesame oil**
- Pinch of **granulated sugar**

for the pancakes

- ½ cup **all-purpose flour**
- ½ cup **potato starch, white rice flour,** or **cornstarch**
- ¾ teaspoon **fine sea salt**, plus more for sprinkling
- ½ teaspoon **baking powder**
- ¾ cup **ice-cold water**
- 1 large **egg**
- ¼ cup finely chopped **kimchi**
- 4 cups shredded **mixed raw vegetables** (carrots, zucchini, bell peppers, kale, whatever you've got; see Kitchen Decoder, page 18)
- 4 **scallions** (white and green parts), thinly sliced
- 2 tablespoons **grapeseed oil** or **peanut oil**, plus more as needed
- **Hot sauce,** for serving (optional)

get it set

Line a plate with a double layer of paper towels and place it next to the stove to hold the cooked pajeon.

Heat the oven to 250°F unless you want to serve the pajeon as they cook (see Step 5).

Set out all your ingredients.

1. Make the dipping sauce: In a small bowl, stir together the soy sauce, vinegar, ginger or garlic if using, sesame oil, and sugar. Set aside until serving time (it can sit out for up to 4 hours).

2. Make the pancakes: In a large bowl, whisk together the all-purpose flour, potato starch, salt, and baking powder.

3. In a medium bowl, whisk together the cold water, egg, and kimchi. Whisk the egg mixture into the flour mixture until smooth, then fold in the shredded vegetables and about three-quarters of the scallions (save some scallions for garnish).

(recipe continues)

4. Place a large, preferably nonstick, skillet over medium-high heat, then add the oil and let it heat up for about 20 seconds. It will shimmer and thin out as it heats, but it shouldn't get hot enough to start to smoke (if it does, move the pan off the heat for a few seconds). Scoop ¼-cup portions of the batter into the skillet, forming as many pancakes as will fit in the skillet without touching. Flatten them with a spatula, and fry until they are dark golden on the bottom, 2 to 3 minutes.

5. Flip them and continue to fry until the other side is browned and crispy, another 2 to 4 minutes. If the pancakes start to get too dark, reduce the heat. As the pancakes cook, transfer them to the paper towel–lined plate and sprinkle them lightly with salt. Continue with the remaining batter, using more oil as needed. You can either serve the pajeon immediately after each batch is cooked, or put the plate in the preheated oven to keep warm while you cook the rest.

6. Sprinkle the reserved sliced scallions over the pancakes and serve with the dipping sauce, and with hot sauce if you like.

tips & tweaks   ● If you have leftover vegetables in the fridge—sautéed greens or roasted veggies—you can use those instead of the raw vegetables. Just chop them up before adding them to the batter in Step 3.

Chicken Enchiladas, Chock-full of Cheese

Tangy tomato-jalapeño sauce, gooey cheese, and lots of creamy sour cream: that's the whole enchilada. You don't need to serve this with anything more than, say, a lemony seltzer for sipping, but for some velvety freshness, try topping the enchiladas with some slices of ripe avocado, sprinkled with a little salt and drizzled with fresh lime juice. This is not *strictly* a one-pot dish, but it's as easy as one.

2 tablespoons **extra-virgin olive oil**

1 medium **red onion,** diced (see Onion Prep, page 12)

2 **garlic cloves,** minced (see Garlic Prep, page 13)

2 tablespoons chopped **fresh cilantro,** plus more for serving

1 teaspoon **chili powder**

1 (28-ounce) can **diced tomatoes** with their juices

¼ cup **pickled jalapeño slices** with liquid (store-bought or see page 48), plus more for garnish if you like

Kosher salt and **freshly ground black pepper**

3 cups diced **cooked chicken,** homemade (from one of the chicken recipes on pages 106 to 113) or from a store-bought rotisserie chicken

12 (6-inch) fresh **corn tortillas**

1½ cups **sour cream** or plain yogurt, plus ½ cup for serving

2 cups / 8 ounces shredded **Monterey Jack cheese**

Sliced **avocado,** sprinkled with salt and drizzled with **lime juice,** for serving (optional)

get it set

Heat the oven to 375°F.

Set out all your ingredients.

1. Make the enchilada sauce: Heat a large skillet over medium heat, then add the oil and let it heat up for about 20 seconds. It will shimmer and thin out as it heats, but it shouldn't get hot enough to start to smoke (if it does, move the pan off the heat immediately for a few seconds). Stir in the onion and garlic, and sauté until you can smell them, about 3 minutes. Keep an eye on it—garlic burns really quickly. Then stir in the cilantro and chili powder. Add the tomatoes with their juices and 2 tablespoons of the liquid from the jalapeños. Simmer the enchilada sauce until it begins to thicken, about 6 minutes. Taste, and season with salt and pepper as needed.

2. In a bowl, combine the cooked chicken, pickled jalapeños, and 2 cups of the enchilada sauce.

3. Spread ½ cup of the enchilada sauce over bottom of a 9 x 13-inch baking dish.

4. Heat a small dry skillet over medium heat. Heat 1 tortilla in the skillet, just to soften it so that it will roll up and stay closed easily at the end of this step, about 10 seconds per side (use tongs to flip it). Transfer the tortilla to a work surface and use a spoon to smear about a heaping tablespoon of the sour cream in the center. Top that with ¼ cup of the chicken filling, sprinkle with a heaping tablespoon grated cheese, and roll it up. Place the enchilada, seam-side down, on top of the sauce in the baking dish. Repeat, making 11 more enchiladas. Spoon the remaining sauce over the enchiladas and sprinkle the remaining cheese on top. Cover the pan with foil.

5. Bake until heated through, 15 to 20 minutes. Uncover the pan and top the enchiladas with dollops of the remaining sour cream. Garnish with avocado, cilantro, and pickled jalapeños if you like.

tips & tweaks

● Make this vegetarian by using seitan or baked tofu in place of the chicken.

● You can add a little sweetness by tossing a cup of raisins (either golden or black) in with the filling in Step 2.

Breads

Pumpkin or Banana Bread—Or Is It Cake??

MAKES 1 LOAF, 8 TO 10 SLICES

Welcome to an amazing alternate universe where bread and cake are the *same thing*. This recipe works with mashed-up ripe bananas or canned pumpkin, so you can make the one you like best (or try both!). Bake it for snacking, then toast and butter a slice for breakfast the next morning.

(See Weigh It Up, page 13.)

1 cup / 225 grams canned **pumpkin puree** (see Tips & Tweaks), or 1 cup / 300 grams mashed ripe banana (from 3 to 4 bananas)

¾ cup / 150 grams **dark brown sugar**

½ cup **sunflower, grapeseed,** or **canola oil**

⅓ cup / 85 grams **plain whole-milk yogurt, sour cream,** or **buttermilk**

2 large **eggs**

2 teaspoons / 8 grams **vanilla extract**

1½ teaspoons / 6 grams **baking powder**

1 teaspoon / 4 grams **baking soda**

¾ teaspoon / 4 grams **kosher salt**

1¾ cups / 220 grams **all-purpose flour**

Cinnamon sugar (see page 222), for sprinkling (optional)

get it set

Heat the oven to 350°F.

Butter a 9 x 5-inch loaf pan.

Set out all your ingredients.

1. In a large bowl, combine the pumpkin or banana, brown sugar, oil, yogurt, eggs, and vanilla. Whisk until the mixture is smooth and all the brown sugar lumps have dissolved, about 1 minute.

2. Whisk in the baking powder, baking soda, and salt until smooth. Then whisk in the flour and any spices you like (see Tips & Tweaks), or leave out the spices altogether.

3. Scrape the batter into the buttered loaf pan and sprinkle the top with cinnamon sugar, if using. Bake for 45 to 60 minutes, until the top of the bread springs back when lightly pressed with a finger and a cake tester or toothpick inserted all the way into the center comes out without any batter clinging to it.

4. Transfer the pan to a wire rack to cool. When it has fully cooled, turn the bread out of the pan and serve.

tips & tweaks

● You don't need the entire can of pumpkin to make this bread, so freeze the extra until the next time you're ready to bake. It will keep for 1 year.

● For some crunch, fold ½ cup chocolate chips or chopped nuts into the batter (do this at Step 2).

● Spice it up! Add up to 1¼ teaspoons total of any combination of

- Cinnamon
- Ginger
- Allspice
- Cardamom
- Nutmeg
- Pumpkin pie spice
- Cloves (no more than a small pinch)

Crispy Skillet Cornbread

SERVES 6 TO 8

Slather this cornbread with butter and then drizzle it with honey. Heaven. The screaming-hot cast-iron pan you bake it in turns the edges golden-crispy and makes for a soft and tender center. It goes great with chili, but you will want it for breakfast, too. If you're eating it the next day, just put it in the toaster oven for a few minutes to bring it back to life.

(See Weigh It Up, page 13.)

1 cup / 120 grams fine or medium **yellow cornmeal**

⅔ cup / 85 grams **all-purpose flour**

1 tablespoon / 15 grams **baking powder**

1¼ teaspoons / 7 grams **kosher salt**

1 cup / 240 grams **sour cream** or whole-milk Greek yogurt

½ cup / 123 grams **whole milk**

⅓ cup / 113 grams **honey**, plus more for serving

2 large **eggs**

¼ teaspoon **baking soda**

8 tablespoons / 1 stick / 113 grams **unsalted butter**, plus more for serving

get it set

Heat the oven to 375°F.

Set out all your ingredients.

Take out oven mitts.

1. In a large bowl, whisk together the cornmeal, flour, baking powder, and salt.

2. In a medium bowl, whisk together the sour cream, milk, honey, eggs, and baking soda. Gently fold this mixture into the cornmeal mixture, folding until everything is combined and there's no flour in the bottom of the bowl.

3. Place a 9-inch cast-iron skillet over high heat on the stovetop until it gets really hot, about 5 minutes. (Keep oven mitts handy for the hot handle! If you forget and grab it, you will end up with a very nasty burn.) Add the butter to the skillet and let it melt. Using those oven mitts to protect your hands, move the pan gently in a circular motion to coat the bottom and sides with melted butter. Turn off the heat and carefully pour the batter into the skillet, using a whisk to combine it with the butter (just a few stirs will do it).

4. Wearing the mitts, put the pan in the oven and bake until the top is golden and a toothpick inserted into the center comes out clean, 25 to 30 minutes.

5. Serve the cornbread warm, slathered with butter and drizzled with more honey.

tips & tweaks

● To give the cornbread a butterscotch-y flavor, brown the butter: After the butter has melted in the skillet in Step 3, reduce the heat to low and keep cooking it over low heat until it stops bubbling, the white foam falls to the bottom and turns golden brown, and the butter smells nutty (this takes 2 to 3 minutes). Then add the batter and continue with the recipe.

Fluffy Buttermilk Biscuits Put a Spell on You

Why, of all the breads, are oven-fresh biscuits so irresistible? They sit on the plate all warm, light, fluffy, flaky. Surely it can't hurt to put some butter on one of them, and maybe some jam? But alas, soon you're in a trance, no longer responsible for your actions, and the second biscuit has vanished! Just try not to eat the whole batch yourself, okay?

(See Weigh It Up, page 13.)

1½ cups / 190 grams **all-purpose flour,** plus more for the counter

2 teaspoons **granulated sugar**

1 teaspoon / 6 grams **kosher salt**

1 teaspoon / 5 grams **baking soda**

½ teaspoon / 3 grams **baking powder**

8 tablespoons / 1 stick / 113 grams *really cold* **unsalted butter,** cut into 16 even slices (see Tips & Tweaks)

⅔ to ¾ cup / 160 to 180 grams **buttermilk** or plain whole-milk yogurt

Melted **unsalted butter,** heavy cream, or milk, for brushing

get it set

Heat the oven to 425°F.

Line a sheet pan with parchment paper or a nonstick liner, or lightly grease it.

Have a ruler at the ready for measuring the thickness of the dough.

Set out all your ingredients.

1. In a large bowl, whisk together the flour, sugar, salt, baking soda, and baking powder.

2. Add the cold butter slices to the bowl. Use your fingers to smush the butter into the flour, tossing and breaking up the butter into pea-size pieces and pressing them into disks between your fingers. You want to end up with what looks like a bowl of floury butter flakes (in fact, it is exactly a bowl of floury butter flakes, and those flakes bake into a light and crispy biscuit). Don't overwork it–it should be shaggy. Overworking the dough will soften the butter in the warmth of your hands, which means fewer flakes and less fluffiness, and you want fluffiness.

(recipe continues)

3. Make a well like a volcano crater in the center of the flour mixture, and pour in ⅔ cup of the buttermilk. Stir the mixture together until it just forms a soft, sticky dough with visible pieces of butter sticking out. If the dough seems dry and floury, add another tablespoon or so of buttermilk, up to ¾ cup total.

4. Sprinkle a little flour on your clean countertop or other work surface and turn the dough out onto it. Knead two or three times (see How to Knead Dough, page 223),

then pat it out into an even ¾-inch-thick rectangle. Fold the dough over itself so it's 1½ inches thick. Use a pastry brush to lightly coat the dough with melted butter, cream, or plain milk (this will help turn the tops of the biscuits golden brown).

5. Cut the dough into 2-inch squares and place them, buttered-side up, on the prepared sheet pan. Bake until the biscuits have puffed up and are deep brown on top and biscuit-y, 12 to 18 minutes. Serve hot or warm.

tips & tweaks

● The first rule of Flaky Biscuit Club: Keep that butter cold! The cold bits of butter slowly release steam in the oven, and that steam is what causes the flakes. If you work the butter so much that it starts to melt from the warmth of your hands, the biscuits won't puff up nearly as much. If the butter does start to soften, just stick the bowl in the fridge for 20 minutes or so to let it get cold again. Then continue with your smushing, maybe a little more gently and quickly.

● Want a nuttier-tasting biscuit? Substitute a little (up to ½ cup) whole-wheat flour, or spelt or rye flour, for the same amount of all-purpose flour.

Rise Up!
The Science of Bread

Here's how to transform yeast, water, flour, and salt into bread, step by step:

activate the yeast

When you add yeast to a liquid with sugar (or something that contains sugars), the yeast starts eating the sugar and releasing gas. (Burping? Farting? Hard to describe exactly what's going on in that bowl.) You'll see the gas create a bit of foam after a few minutes. Now that the yeast is awake, you can add the flour and other ingredients, such as salt.

knead the dough

You can use the dough hook attachment of a stand mixer, or you can knead by hand (see How to Knead Dough, page 223). Flour is made from wheat, which contains a complex mix of proteins (long molecular chains built from amino acids) called gluten. When water is added to flour, the gluten proteins form long strands that stick to each other. Kneading distributes the ingredients evenly, and gives the dough structure by folding a pattern of these gluten strands back on itself, creating a 3D gluten network. Think of it as a mass of tiny balloons that will be inflated by the gas the yeast will produce during rising and baking. This is what makes bread light, instead of brick-like. You know your dough has been kneaded enough when all the flour is incorporated and it feels springy and elastic. If you pull it, it will stretch.

let the dough rise

The yeast will continue to eat and release gas, inflating those balloons you made when you kneaded it.

After letting the dough rise, you punch it down. You're deflating the dough to let it reinflate even more. By pressing out the gas from the first rise, you stretch and thin out the gluten membrane, making it more flexible. It's like when you stretch a rubber balloon to make it easier to blow up. This helps the dough rise even higher when it's in the oven and makes the center nice and soft.

Let it rise again, bigger.

bake

During baking, the yeast releases even more gas, creating the final air pockets in your bread. When you slice it, you can see them— those same balloons that you created by kneading, inflated by yeast, and now ready to eat. Thanks, yeast!

Best Squishy White Bread

MAKES 2 LOAVES

The squishy white bread of your dreams: soft, a little sweet, perfect for sandwiches or toasting and buttering. This recipe makes two loaves: one for now, and one for the freezer. The frozen loaf will defrost on the counter in about 2 hours, meaning if you take it out in the morning, it will be ready in time for lunch (grilled cheese! PB&J!).

(See Weigh It Up, page 13.)

1 packet / 2½ teaspoons / 7 grams **active dry yeast** (or 1¾ teaspoons / 5 grams instant yeast)

3 tablespoons / 42 grams **granulated sugar**, divided

1½ cups / 355 mL **lukewarm milk** (it should feel slightly warm but not at all hot when you stick your finger into it), divided

1 tablespoon / 15 grams **kosher salt**

4 tablespoons / ½ stick / 57 grams **unsalted butter**, melted, divided, plus more for the pans and bowl

2 large **eggs**

5 to 6 cups / 625 to 750 grams **all-purpose flour**, plus more for the work surface

get it set

Brush a large bowl for the dough with melted butter.

Generously grease two 9 x 5-inch loaf pans with melted butter.

If you have an electric stand mixer, fit it with the paddle attachment and have the dough hook at the ready. (Or you can use a large bowl and a wooden spoon.)

Set out all your ingredients.

1. Activate the yeast and blend the ingredients: In the bowl of an electric stand mixer or another large bowl, dissolve the yeast and a pinch of the sugar in ¼ cup of the warm milk. Let the mixture sit for a few minutes, until it starts to get a little frothy; that's the yeast getting active. Using the paddle attachment or a wooden spoon, mix in the remaining 1¼ cups warm milk, the remaining sugar, the salt, 3 tablespoons of the butter, and the eggs until combined, about 1 minute. Add 5 cups (625 grams) of the flour and mix until smooth, another 2 minutes with the mixer or 4 minutes by hand (feel free to abandon the wooden spoon and use your hands at this point, as the dough may be hard to mix).

2. Knead the dough: Switch to the dough hook attachment and knead on low speed, adding more flour if necessary, until the dough is stiff and slightly tacky to the touch, 7 to 10 minutes. Most of the dough will end up wrapped around the dough hook and that is okay. You know it's ready when it stretches without tearing easily. You can pause the mixer and pull the dough to test when to stop kneading it.

If you are kneading by hand: Flour a clean work surface, dump the dough onto it, and knead it energetically, leaning your weight into it (see How To Knead Dough, page 223). Stretch it out, then fold it back on itself. Give it a quarter turn and do it again, repeating until the dough reaches the stretchiness described above. It will take about 15 minutes, and it's fun to feel the dough changing in your hands (veteran slime makers will notice a similarity). Keep adding flour bit by bit until the dough is slightly sticky, but not so sticky that your hands are covered with it. You shouldn't need to add more than 1 cup / 125 grams flour to the 5 cups you already used in Step 1.

3. Let the dough rise: Put the dough in the greased bowl and turn it over so the greased side is up. Cover the bowl with a large plate, a pot lid, or plastic wrap and set it in a warm, draft-free spot until the dough has doubled in size, 1½ to 3 hours.

4. When the dough has doubled in size, turn it out onto a floured surface and knead it for 3 minutes. Return the dough to the greased bowl, cover the bowl, and let it rise again for 30 minutes.

5. Press down on the dough with your hand to expel the air and deflate the dough. Divide the dough in half and place each half into a greased loaf pan. Brush the tops of the loaves with the remaining 1 tablespoon melted butter.

6. Cover the pans with clean kitchen towels or plastic wrap, and let the dough rise until it is just above the tops of the pans, 45 minutes to 1 hour.

7. Meanwhile, heat the oven to 400°F.

8. Bake the bread: When the dough is done rising, put the loaf pans in the oven and bake for 10 minutes. Then reduce the heat to 350°F and bake for an additional 20 to 30 minutes, until the loaves sound hollow when tapped and their tops are golden brown. If you have an instant-read thermometer, stick the probe in the center of a loaf (go in from the side or the bottom so the top still looks nice); the internal temperature should be about 200°F. Remove the loaves from the pans and let them cool completely on wire racks; this will take about 2 hours.

9. When the bread is completely cool, you can slice it.

Rise & Dine
Cinnamon Raisin Bread

Warm waves of cinnamon aroma can lift you right out of any dull routine. You'll make two loaves here: eat one warm from the oven, or toasted and buttered the next day. Freeze the other loaf and use it to make the best French toast ever (page 36).

(See Weigh It Up, page 13.)

1 packet /
2½ teaspoons /
7 grams **active dry yeast** (or 1¾ teaspoons /
5 grams instant yeast)

⅓ cup / 67 grams **granulated sugar,** divided

1½ cups / 355 mL **lukewarm milk** (it should feel slightly warm but not at all hot when you stick your finger into it), divided

1 tablespoon /
15 grams **kosher salt**

7 tablespoons /
105 grams **unsalted butter,** melted, divided, plus more for the pans and bowl

2 large **eggs**

5 to 6 cups /
625 to 750 grams **all-purpose flour,** plus more for the work surface

⅓ cup / 79 mL **orange juice** or apple cider

1½ cups / 225 grams golden or dark **raisins**

½ cup / 100 grams **dark brown sugar**

1 tablespoon /
8 grams **ground cinnamon**

Cinnamon sugar, for dusting (see Tips & Tweaks, page 222)

get it set

Brush a large bowl for the dough with melted butter.

Generously grease two 9 x 5-inch loaf pans with melted butter.

If you have an electric stand mixer, fit it with the paddle attachment and have the dough hook at the ready. (Or you can use a large bowl and wooden spoon.)

Set out all your ingredients.

1. Activate the yeast and blend the wet ingredients: In the bowl of an electric stand mixer or another large bowl, dissolve the yeast and a pinch of the sugar in ¼ cup of the warm milk. Let the mixture sit until it starts to bubble; that's the yeast getting active. Using the paddle attachment (or a wooden spoon), mix in the remaining 1¼ cups warm milk, remaining sugar, salt, 3 tablespoons of the butter, and the eggs. Add the flour and mix until smooth, 2 minutes with the mixer or 4 minutes by hand (feel free to abandon the wooden spoon and use your hands at this point, as the dough may be hard to mix).

(recipe continues)

2. Knead the dough: Switch to the dough hook attachment and knead on low speed, adding more flour if necessary, until the dough is stiff and slightly tacky to the touch, 7 to 10 minutes. Most of the dough will end up wrapped around the dough hook and that is okay. You know it's ready when it stretches without tearing easily.

If you are kneading by hand: Flour a clean work surface, dump the dough onto it, and knead it energetically, leaning your weight into it (see How to Knead Dough, page 223). Stretch it out, then fold it back on itself. Give it a quarter turn and do it again, repeating until the dough reaches the stretchiness described above. It will take about 15 minutes, and it's fun to feel the dough changing in your hands (veteran slime makers will notice a similarity). Keep adding flour bit by bit until the dough is slightly sticky, but not so sticky that your hands are covered with it. You shouldn't need to add more than 1 cup / 125 grams flour to the 5 cups you already used in Step 1.

3. Let the dough rise: Put the dough in the greased bowl and turn it over so the greased side is up. Cover the bowl with a large plate, a pot lid, or plastic wrap and set it in a warm, draft-free spot until the dough has doubled in size, 1½ to 3 hours.

4. Meanwhile, in a small pot, bring the orange juice to a simmer, and let it cook until it has reduced by half, 8 to 10 minutes. Remove it from the heat, add the raisins, cover the pot, and let it sit until it is needed for the filling in Step 6.

5. When the dough has doubled in size, turn it out onto a floured surface and knead it for 3 minutes. Return the dough to the greased bowl, cover the bowl, and let it rise again for 30 minutes.

6. Divide the dough in half and roll one half into an 8 x 16-inch rectangle. Brush the top with 1 tablespoon melted butter. Drain the raisins, discarding the liquid, put them in a small bowl, and mix them with the brown sugar and cinnamon. Scatter half of the raisin

tips & tweaks

● To make **Cinnamon Sugar,** mix together 2 teaspoons granulated sugar and ½ teaspoon ground cinnamon.

● Add a **Coconut Dulce de Leche Filling:** Skip the raisin mixture and the melted butter in the filling, and instead spread each portion of dough with a generous ⅓ cup dulce de leche and ½ cup unsweetened coconut flakes. Roll up and continue with the recipe.

● You could also use Nutella instead of dulce de leche to make a chocolate coconut bread.

mixture over the dough. Starting from one of the short ends, roll it up tightly, tucking the ends under. Place the roll seam-side down in a greased loaf pan and brush the top with another tablespoon of melted butter; dust it with cinnamon sugar. Repeat with remaining dough.

7. Cover the pans with clean kitchen towels or plastic wrap, and let the dough rise until it is just above the tops of the pans, 45 minutes to 1 hour.

8. Meanwhile, heat the oven to 400°F.

9. **Bake the bread:** When the dough is done rising, put the pans in the oven and bake for 10 minutes. Then reduce the heat to 350°F and bake for an additional 20 to 30 minutes, until the loaves are golden brown and sound hollow when tapped. If you have an instant-read thermometer, stick the probe in the center of the loaf (go in from the side or bottom so the top still looks nice); the internal temperature should be about 200°F. Remove the loaves from the pans and let them cool on wire racks; this takes about 2 hours.

10. When the loaves have cooled, you can slice them.

how to knead dough

Kneading dough is the second most satisfying thing when it comes to bread baking. (The first, of course, is breaking into the finished loaf and slathering it with butter.) The rhythmic motion and the feel of the dough can be fun and relaxing.

1. Sprinkle a flat, smooth work surface with just enough flour to keep the dough from sticking. Scrape the dough out of the bowl with your hands, a spatula, or a dough scraper, and put it on the work surface.

2. Begin kneading by gently pressing the dough down and away from you with the heels of your hands. (If your hands stick to the dough, rub some flour on them.) In one confident, swift motion, lift the edge of the dough that's farthest away from you and fold the dough in half toward you.

3. Turn the dough 45 degrees and knead it again with the heels of your hands. If it gets sticky, add a little more flour to the work surface or your hands. (Be stingy, though, because adding too much flour at this stage can result in tough bread.)

4. Continue to knead, fold, and turn the dough until it is smooth and elastic. It should feel stretchy when you pull it. Depending on the kind of dough, this can take from 4 to 20 minutes.

Whole-Wheat Honey Bread

MAKES 2 LOAVES

A touch of sweetness is all it takes to get along with almost anyone. This bread goes with butter, jam, cheese, or whatever you want to spread on it. It's earthy from the whole-wheat flour, friendly from the honey, and just as soft as you like it. A dash of buckwheat flour adds a deep, almost spicy note.

(See Weigh It Up, page 13.)

1 packet / 2½ teaspoons / 7 grams **active dry yeast** (or 1¾ teaspoons / 5 grams instant yeast)

Pinch of **granulated sugar**

1½ cups / 355 mL **lukewarm milk** (it should feel slightly warm but not at all hot when you stick your finger into it), divided

2 tablespoons / 43 grams **honey**

1 tablespoon / 15 grams **kosher salt**

4 tablespoons / ½ stick / 99 grams **unsalted butter**, melted, plus more for the pans and bowl

2 large **eggs**

2 cups / 260 grams **whole-wheat flour**

2 tablespoons / 15 grams **buckwheat flour** (optional; or use more whole-wheat)

3 to 4 cups / 375 to 500 grams **all-purpose flour**, plus more for the work surface

get it set

Brush a large bowl for the dough with melted butter.

Generously grease two 9 x 5-inch loaf pans with melted butter.

If you have an electric stand mixer, fit it with the paddle attachment and have the dough hook at the ready. (Or you can use a large bowl and wooden spoon.)

Set out all your ingredients.

1. Activate the yeast and blend the ingredients: In the bowl of an electric stand mixer or another large bowl, dissolve the yeast and the sugar in ¼ cup of the warm milk. Let the mixture sit for a few minutes, until it starts to get a little frothy; that's the yeast getting active. Using the paddle attachment or a wooden spoon, mix in the remaining 1¼ cups warm milk, the honey, the salt, 3 tablespoons of the butter, and the eggs until combined, about 1 minute. Add all the whole-wheat flour, the buckwheat flour if using, and 3 cups / 375 grams of the all-purpose flour and mix until smooth, another 2 minutes with the mixer or 4 minutes by hand (feel free to abandon the wooden spoon and use your hands at this point, as the dough may be hard to mix).

2. Knead the dough: Switch to the dough hook attachment and knead on low speed, adding more all-purpose flour if necessary, until the dough is stiff and slightly tacky to the touch, 7 to 10 minutes. Most of the dough will end up wrapped around the dough hook and that is okay. You know it's ready when it stretches without tearing easily. You can pause the mixer and pull the dough glob to test when to stop kneading it.

If you are kneading by hand: Flour a clean work surface, dump the dough onto it, and knead it energetically, leaning your weight into it (see How to Knead Dough, page 223). Stretch it out, then fold it back on itself. Give it a quarter turn and do it again, repeating until the dough reaches the stretchiness described above. It will take about 15 minutes. Keep adding all-purpose flour bit by bit until the dough is slightly sticky, but not so sticky that your hands are covered with it. You shouldn't need to add more than 1 cup / 125 grams all-purpose flour to the 5 cups you already used in Step 1.

3. Let the dough rise: Put the dough in the greased bowl and turn it over so the greased side is up. Cover the bowl with a large plate, a pot lid, or plastic wrap, and set it in a warm, draft-free spot until the dough has doubled in size, 1½ to 3 hours.

4. When the dough has doubled in size, turn it out onto a floured surface and knead it for 3 minutes. Return the dough to the greased bowl, cover the bowl, and let it rise again for 30 minutes.

5. Press down on the dough with your hand to expel the air and deflate the dough. Divide the dough in half and place each half into a greased loaf pan. Brush the tops of the loaves with the remaining 1 tablespoon melted butter.

6. Cover the loaf pans with clean kitchen towels or plastic wrap, and let the dough rise until it is just above the tops of the pans, 45 minutes to 1 hour.

7. Meanwhile, heat the oven to 400°F.

8. Bake the bread: When the dough is done rising, put the pans in the oven and bake for 10 minutes. Then reduce the heat to 350°F and bake for an additional 20 to 30 minutes, until the loaves sound hollow when tapped and the tops are golden brown. If you have an instant-read thermometer, stick the probe in the center of the loaf (go in from the side or bottom so the top still looks nice); the internal temperature should be about 200°F. Remove the loaves from the pans and let them cool completely on wire racks; this will take about 2 hours.

9. When the bread is completely cool, you can slice it.

Citrusy Olive Oil Challah

Great challah is pillow-soft and slightly sweet in flavor. The loaf is traditionally made with an egg-enriched dough. Here, extra-virgin olive oil makes this challah even richer, and a little bit of grated orange zest plus orange juice makes it tangy. Unlike white and whole-wheat bread doughs, which call for all-purpose flour, this one uses bread flour, which creates a stronger dough that is easy to braid.

(See Weigh It Up, page 13.)

2 medium **oranges,** at room temperature

1 packet / 2½ teaspoons / 7 grams **active dry yeast**

⅓ cup / 78 mL **extra-virgin olive oil,** plus more for the pan and bowl

3 large **eggs,** at room temperature

1 large **egg yolk,** at room temperature

3 tablespoons / 37 grams **granulated sugar**

1 teaspoon / 6 grams **kosher salt**

3 to 3½ cups / 375 to 440 grams **bread flour,** plus more for kneading the dough

get it set

If you store oranges in the fridge, take them out 30 to 60 minutes in advance to let them warm to room temperature.

Brush a large bowl for the dough with olive oil.

Grease a large sheet pan with olive oil or line it with parchment paper.

If you have an electric stand mixer, fit it with the paddle attachment and have the dough hook at the ready. (Or you can use a large bowl and a wooden spoon.)

Set out all your ingredients.

1. Using a Microplane or other fine grater, finely grate ½ teaspoon zest from one of the oranges and set it aside.

2. **Activate the yeast:** Squeeze the juice from both oranges into a measuring cup to yeild ½ cup (if it's less than that, add water; if it's more than that, drink the rest). Pour the juice into the bowl of an electric stand mixer or another large bowl. Sprinkle the yeast over the juice and let it sit until it becomes frothy; that's the yeast getting active.

(recipe continues)

3. Blend the ingredients: Using the paddle attachment or a wooden spoon, mix in the oil, 2 eggs, the egg yolk, and the sugar, salt, and orange zest until just combined, about 1 minute. Switch to a dough hook if you are using a mixer, and mix in the flour, 1 cup at a time. (Or use your hands to do this if you are working in a bowl.) You may or may not use all of the flour, so at the end, add it gradually, stopping when the dough turns into a sticky, cohesive mass.

4. Knead the dough: Transfer the dough and any floury bits at the bottom of the bowl to a floured work surface and knead until smooth, about 5 minutes. Put the dough in the greased bowl and turn it over so the greased side is up. Cover the bowl with a large plate, a pot lid, or plastic wrap, and set it in a warm, draft-free spot until the dough has doubled in size, 1½ to 3 hours.

5. Press down on the dough to expel the air, deflating it. Cover the bowl again, and let the dough rise for another 45 minutes. It will be puffed looking, but not doubled in size.

6. Form the loaf and let it rise: In a small bowl, combine the remaining 1 egg with 1 teaspoon water to make the egg wash. To make a classic braided challah, see How to Braid a Challah, opposite (see Tips & Tweaks for a round challah). Place the formed loaf on the greased sheet pan, and brush it all over with the egg wash (reserve the unused egg wash). Let it rise, uncovered, for 45 minutes.

7. Meanwhile, place a rack in the middle position and heat the oven to 375°F.

8. Gently brush a second coat of the egg wash over the dough, put the sheet pan in the oven, and bake the challah for 25 to 35 minutes, until it is a deep rich brown and the bottom sounds hollow when tapped. (Stay alert! When it starts smelling like freshly baked bread, start checking.) Let the challah cool completely on a wire rack, about 2 hours, before serving.

---

tips & tweaks

● Don't substitute commercial orange juice for freshly squeezed. Some packaged orange juices have preservatives in them that can prevent the yeast from activating.

● You can make a round challah instead of a braid: Form the dough into a single thick rope about 12 inches long, and spiral it into a round (think snail shell). Tuck the end underneath, brush with the egg wash, and bake as directed for the braid.

● For a more traditional challah, substitute a neutral oil such as sunflower or grapeseed for the olive oil, substitute water for the orange juice, and leave out the zest.

How to Braid a Challah

Challah can be shaped in many ways, but the most traditional is a 3-strand braid.

Cut the dough: Divide the challah dough into 3 equal portions. Use a kitchen scale if you want to be precise about it; otherwise, you can do this by sight and feel.

Shape the dough: Lightly flour your hands and the work surface. Shape and gently stretch each piece of dough to form a log shape. Roll each log on the work surface until it begins to look like a rope, about 12 inches long. Apply even pressure when rolling out the dough ropes to achieve even thickness.

Assemble the dough: On a piece of parchment paper or a lightly oiled sheet pan, line up the dough ropes vertically, side by side, with about an inch of space between them. If one of your ropes is thinner or thicker than the two others, make that the center strand. At the top end, firmly pinch the ends of the 3 dough ropes together. Tuck the pinched-together ends underneath to help hold them together while you braid.

Braid the dough: If you've ever braided hair, it's like that. Lift the dough rope on the right over the center rope and place it between the center and left strands. The rope that *was* on the right now becomes the center rope, *and the original center rope is now on the right.* Now lift the dough rope on the left over the new center strand and place it between the center and right strands. The rope that had been on the left is now in the center. Proceed using this same pattern. Try to keep the braid fairly tight as you work your way down. Once you've come to the bottom of the loaf, pinch the ends of the ropes together, and tuck them under the way you did at the top of the loaf. That's it!

Sides

Buttery Mashed Potato Cloud

SERVES 6

The joke around my house is that the secret ingredient is always butter. (Which isn't even true—it's usually anchovies.) Yukon Gold potatoes taste buttery all by themselves, so adding actual butter to them creates something like a warm butter cloud that you can eat (other potatoes work great, too). I add buttermilk for tang and a little nutmeg for a note of sweet spiciness. Peel the potatoes if you prefer a perfectly smooth mash, or leave them on because the skin adds texture and flavor. (Wait, come to think of it, why not add some anchovies? See Tips & Tweaks.) Choose your own cloud nine!

3 pounds **Yukon Gold** or other potatoes, peeled or not, cut into 2-inch chunks

Kosher salt, as needed

⅓ cup **buttermilk** (or use milk or half-and-half)

6 tablespoons / ⅔ stick / 85 grams **unsalted butter**, cut into chunks, at room temperature

¼ teaspoon **freshly ground black pepper**

⅛ teaspoon freshly grated **nutmeg**

get it set

Put a colander or strainer in the sink for draining the potatoes.

Set out all your ingredients.

1. Put the potatoes in a large pot with enough salted water to cover them. Make sure the pot has enough room over the water line so it won't boil over, at least 2 inches. Bring to a boil over high heat, then reduce the heat to medium. Simmer until the potatoes are very tender when pierced with the tip of a paring knife, 12 to 18 minutes. Drain the potatoes in the colander or strainer.

2. Put the empty pot back on the stove and add the buttermilk, butter, 1 teaspoon salt, the pepper, and the nutmeg. Bring the mixture to a simmer and immediately add the potatoes. Remove from the heat.

3. Use a potato masher or a fork to mash everything together in the pot. Taste, and add more salt if needed. Serve immediately.

● Mashing the potatoes in the pot, with either a potato masher or a fork, is the easiest and fastest way to get the job done. A masher leaves some lumps, which I like. For smooth, silky mashed potatoes, use a food mill or a potato ricer. A food processor will also work in a pinch, but it can make the potatoes somewhat gluey.

● **Cheesy Mashed Potatoes** might be one of the few ways to improve on the regular version. To make them, add ½ to 1 cup shredded cheddar, Monterey Jack, Gruyère, or other firm cheese to the pot when you put the potatoes back in, after you've simmered the buttermilk mixture. The heat of the pot will melt the cheese into the potatoes. A tablespoon or two of chopped chives or parsley is great here, too.

● For a whoosh of stealth umami, add 1 or 2 minced anchovy fillets to the buttermilk mixture before returning the potatoes to the pot for mashing. No one will know they're there while they work their magic. Butter is the secret ingredient, but anchovies are the *secret* secret ingredient.

Roast Any Roastable Vegetable

You don't need a recipe to roast a pan of vegetables—just a technique. And the technique is the same no matter what kind you're cooking, whether a potato or a cherry tomato, broccoli, cauliflower. . . . Grab your favorite veg, let's try it:

1. Cut your vegetables (except cherry tomatoes) into 1-inch pieces. Keeping them the same size means they will cook evenly.

2. Put the vegetables on a rimmed sheet pan and drizzle them with 2 to 4 tablespoons of some kind of oil or fat. I usually use olive oil, but sunflower, grapeseed, canola, and coconut oil all work, as does melted butter, lard, duck fat, or bacon fat. Add just enough oil or fat to coat the vegetables lightly.

3. Spread the veggies out in one layer and sprinkle them with salt. Don't crowd them. Leaving at least ⅛ inch between pieces lets them brown at the edges, rather than getting soggy from the steam from the other pieces (vegetables contain a lot of water). Use two pans if you need to.

4. Add seasonings to the pan. Some possibilities include herb sprigs (thyme, sage, rosemary, marjoram, or bay leaves or whole or ground spices like cumin, paprika, or coriander).

5. Roast according to the timing chart. → Garnish your roasted veggies with a drizzle of olive oil and some chopped fresh herbs if you like. If you want to layer the flavors even more, you can add a dollop of plain yogurt that's been seasoned with a little salt and grated garlic, or spoon on some creamy tahini sauce (see page 136).

vegetables cut into 1-inch chunks unless otherwise noted	cooking time at 425°F
Asparagus, whole	6 to 12 minutes, depending on thickness
Beets	25 to 40 minutes
Bell peppers (red, green, orange)	20 to 30 minutes
Broccoli, in florets	8 to 20 minutes
Brussels sprouts, halved	15 to 25 minutes
Butternut squash / other winter squash	25 to 40 minutes
Carrots, cut into ½-inch chunks, left whole, or halved lengthwise	25 to 40 minutes
Cauliflower florets	20 to 40 minutes
Cherry tomatoes, whole	15 to 25 minutes
Eggplant	20 to 40 minutes
Leeks	15 to 25 minutes
Mushrooms	15 to 25 minutes
Potatoes	25 to 35 minutes
Sweet potatoes or parsnips	25 to 35 minutes
Zucchini / other summer squash	20 to 35 minutes

Browning
How Heat Creates Flavor

Most foods have sugar in them in some form. Fruits obviously, but also vegetables and even meats. When you heat these ingredients, the sugars caramelize, which means they start to break down.

This chemical reaction creates a dark brown color and transforms the sugars' sweetness into a huge, complex collection of new flavors: some sour, some bitter, some intensely aromatic (think of the smell of bread in the toaster).

Plus, if amino acids are present, like those found in onions, potatoes, bread dough, and meats, the result is called a Maillard reaction and adds even more complex flavors, including meaty, floral, and earthy notes.

With both forms of browning–caramelization and Maillard reaction–the more you heat the foods, the more they transform and the more intense they become–ultimately creating that burnt taste we usually try to avoid.

Even though both are browning reactions, when you heat vegetables to the point where they start to brown, it's typically called caramelization (even when it's Maillard, as with onions), and when you do the same thing with meats, it's called browning or searing.

You can caramelize or sear an ingredient in the oven, on the stove, or on a grill–anywhere that uses intense dry heat–or else by frying, which uses a fat like oil or butter to transfer intense heat to the food. A pinch of salt can help release natural sugars, promoting browning. Boiling and poaching do not produce browning, because water cannot get hot enough to cause it (water boils at 212°F, browning begins at 250°F).

Sweet Miso Creamed Corn   SERVES 4

Summer corn doesn't need much help beyond a smear of butter. But corn also lends itself to more exciting dishes, and you can't get much jazzier than this miso-spiked creamed corn. The miso gives it an umami flavor (see Umami, the Fifth Taste, page 202) that's intensified by the garlic and stock. In the middle of the winter you can make it with frozen corn, too. It will warm you right up.

4 ears of **corn**, husked (or 4 cups frozen corn kernels)

⅓ cup **heavy cream**

⅓ cup **chicken** or **vegetable stock** (or water)

1 **fresh thyme sprig** or other woody herb

1 tablespoon **miso paste** (any kind is fine)

1 **garlic clove**, grated (see Garlic Prep, page 13)

Pinch of **cayenne pepper** (optional)

1 tablespoon chopped **fresh mint, cilantro,** or other soft herbs

get it set

Set out all your ingedients.

1. Lay an ear of corn flat on a cutting board and use a sharp paring knife to slice off all the kernels, slicing away from your hands and body and rotating the corn as needed. Repeat with the remaining 3 ears.

2. Put the kernels in a heavy pot and add the cream, stock, and thyme sprig. Bring to a simmer and cook for about 5 minutes, until the kernels are tender. Stir, making sure to scrape the caramelized cream off the sides and bottom of the pan.

3. Remove the pan from the heat, pull out the thyme sprig, and stir in the miso, garlic, and cayenne if using. Let cool for a few minutes before stirring in the chopped herbs and serving.

tips & tweaks

● Laying the corn flat on a cutting board to cut off the kernels keeps the kernels from flying all over the kitchen, which is what happens when you try to slice them off an ear that's held upright.

● You can use all sorts of ingredients to build on this basic recipe. Instead of miso, add bits of crumbled cheese (between 2 tablespoons and ½ cup feta, blue cheese, or goat cheese).

Crumbled cooked bacon and chopped tomatoes also jazz it up. For a carb fest, you could toss this with 8 ounces of cooked whole-wheat couscous or bow ties and make it a main dish.

● You can make a dairy-free version with coconut milk (use the full-fat kind) in place of the cream. It doesn't get quite as thick, but the sweetness is really nice.

Sautéed Greens Remix SERVES 4

(feat. Garlic, Parmesan, and Chile Flakes)

Sautéed greens are a super-easy way to bring something healthy and bright to the table. Using a mix of greens gives the best flavor and texture. One sturdy green like kale or collards, plus one bunch of tender greens, like chard or spinach, creates a perfect mix. The sturdy green keeps some texture while the tender one melts and turns really silky. But it's the crispy slivers of golden garlic that take this to another level. Don't stint on the oil; it makes the whole thing shiny and flavorful. Guaranteed number-one hit.

1 bunch **fresh kale, collard,** or **mustard greens**

1 bunch **fresh spinach** or **chard** (see Tips & Tweaks)

3 tablespoons **extra-virgin olive oil**

2 to 3 **garlic cloves,** thinly sliced (see Garlic Prep, page 13)

Kosher salt or **coarse sea salt**

Pinch of **crushed red pepper flakes**

2 tablespoons **chicken** or **vegetable stock** or water, plus more as needed

½ cup (about 50 grams) **grated Parmesan cheese**

Fresh lemon juice, for serving (optional)

get it set

Set out all your ingredients.

1. Remove the center ribs and center stems from the sturdy greens (kale, collards, or mustard greens) and discard them; tear the leaves into bite-size pieces. Put the greens in a colander and rinse well but do not dry them (you want the moisture on the leaves to help steam them as they cook). Set aside.

Do the same for the tender greens (spinach or chard). If you're using baby spinach, you don't have to remove the stems.

Remember to keep the tender greens (spinach/chard) separate from the sturdy greens (kale/collards/mustard greens).

2. Place a large skillet over medium-high heat, then add the oil and let it heat up for about 20 seconds. It will shimmer and thin out as it heats, but don't let it get hot enough to start to smoke. Stir in the garlic and cook until you can smell it and it's slightly softened, about 1 minute. Add a big pinch of salt and the red pepper flakes, and sauté for another 30 seconds to 1 minute, until the garlic turns very pale gold at the edges (keep an eye on it, and if the garlic starts to get too brown, pull the pan off the heat to let it cool off for a few seconds).

3. Add the damp sturdy greens, a handful at a time, to the garlic in the skillet, letting each handful wilt slightly before adding more; use tongs to toss well. The water will steam off fast and hiss loudly, so you may want to hold the greens at arm's length as you add them. Cook until the greens are wilted but not yet soft, about 5 minutes.

4. Now add the tender greens, also a handful at a time, stirring everything well. Add the stock, and let everything cook for a minute or two more, until all the greens are very soft. If they still seem tough but the pan is dry, splash in a little more water and cook for another few minutes. For very tough greens you might need to repeat this a few times; leathery collard greens can take up to 20 minutes and ½ cup of water to soften, while tender young kale will cook a lot more quickly.

5. Taste, and add more salt if needed. Toss the greens with the cheese and sprinkle with a little lemon juice if you like. Serve hot.

tips & tweaks

● If you are using baby spinach, which is sold by weight and not in a bunch, you'll need 5 to 6 ounces.

● Add 2 to 4 anchovies to the pan along with the garlic. They will melt into the oil and you won't even know they're there, except that the greens will taste richer and saltier, with a lot more oomph.

● Adding a pinch of whole cumin seeds with the garlic gives the greens an earthy flavor. I love it.

Summer Tomatoes
with Pickled Shallots

SERVES 4 TO 6

Summer tomatoes taste like the sweet, warm days they were grown in. It's hard to improve on their elemental flavors. But mixing in pickled shallots adds a shimmering bright taste; fish sauce or soy sauce, a little brininess; and brown sugar, a mild sweetness. Sort of like a beach day on a platter. But don't try this in the winter, because you need ripe summer tomatoes to make it work.

1 small **shallot**, sliced

1 **lime**

½ teaspoon **Asian fish sauce** or soy sauce

½ teaspoon **light** or **dark brown sugar**

Pinch of **crushed red pepper flakes** (optional)

Fine sea salt and **freshly ground black pepper**

2 pounds **ripe tomatoes** (any kind is fine, but a mix of heirlooms will give you the most interesting flavors and colors)

Extra-virgin olive oil, for drizzling

¼ cup torn **fresh soft herbs** like basil, mint, cilantro, or parsley

get it set

Set out all your ingredients.

1. Put the shallot in a small bowl. Using a Microplane or other fine grater, zest the lime into the bowl. Squeeze in the juice from half the lime, saving the other lime half for something else. (Maybe squeeze it into your seltzer?) Add the fish sauce, brown sugar, red pepper flakes if using, and a pinch each of salt and pepper. Let the mixture sit for 5 minutes while you slice the tomatoes.

2. Slice the tomatoes any which way you like—in thick rounds, large chunks, thin wedges, or halved if cherry tomatoes. It's nice to have a variety of textures, so feel free to mix it up. Arrange the tomato pieces on a platter or plate. Scatter the shallots on top, and drizzle with the liquid from the bowl.

3. Drizzle olive oil all over the tomatoes. Top with the herbs and more salt and pepper to taste.

tips & tweaks
● To add crunch, in place of the shallots, slice a sweet Vidalia onion or red onion into rounds and add them to the tomatoes. They have a gentler and less salty taste than the quick-pickled shallots.

Rice, All the Ways

Two-thirds of the world's population eats rice every day, and it's easy to see why. Rice is delicious, widely available, and easy to cook. There are many different kinds of rice and many ways to cook it. We'll focus here on white, brown, and coconut rice, using the most common methods to cook them (cooktop, rice cooker, or other multicooker). Since rice tastes great with almost any other food, learning to cook it right is a skill you'll be glad to master.

MASTER RICE RECIPE
stovetop

MAKES 4 CUPS COOKED RICE, 4 TO 6 SERVINGS

2¾ cups **water**

1½ cups any kind of **white rice** (long- or short-grain), rinsed very well in a strainer

¼ teaspoon **kosher salt**

1. Put the water, rice, and salt in a pot that has a tight-fitting lid. Bring it to a boil, but don't cover the pot yet.

2. Once the water has boiled, cover the pot and reduce the heat to a low simmer. Cook for 15 to 17 minutes, checking on the rice to make sure it's not drying out (if so, reduce the heat). Remove the pot from the heat, place a clean dish towel between the rim of the pot and the lid, and let it stand for 10 minutes to steam (the towel helps absorb excess moisture, making the rice especially fluffy).

tips & tweaks

● To cook **Brown Rice**, use 3 cups water and let the rice cook for 40 to 50 minutes.

● To make **Coconut Rice**, use 1 (13.5-ounce) can of coconut milk and 1 cup of water and let the rice cook for 15 to 17 minutes.

● To make **Coconut Brown Rice**, use 1 (13.5-ounce) can of coconut milk and 1¼ cups of water, and let the rice cook for 40 to 50 minutes.

MASTER RICE RECIPE

electric pressure cooker / instant pot

MAKES 3 CUPS COOKED RICE, 3 OR 4 SERVINGS

This recipe works with any electric pressure cooker or multicooker, and I think it gives slightly better (less mushy) results than using the rice setting found on some appliances. But if you prefer to use the rice setting, follow the manufacturer's instructions.

1 cup any kind of **white rice** (long- or short-grain), rinsed very well in a strainer

1¼ cups **water**

¼ teaspoon **kosher salt**

1. In the insert of the electric pressure cooker, combine the rice, water, and salt.

2. Set the pot to cook on high pressure for 4 minutes for short-grain rice (such as Arborio or sushi rice) or 8 minutes for long-grain rice (jasmine or basmati), then let the pressure release naturally for 10 minutes. Release the remaining pressure manually.

3. Fluff the rice with a fork, then cover the pot with a clean kitchen towel and put the lid back on (loosely, don't lock it in) or place a plate on top of the dish towel. Let it rest for 10 minutes before serving.

tips & tweaks

● To cook **Brown Rice**, cook it on high pressure for 22 minutes, then let the pressure release naturally. Fluff the rice with a fork, then cover the pot with a dish towel and put the lid back on (loosely, don't lock it in) or place a plate on top of the dish towel. Let it rest for 10 minutes before serving.

● To make **Coconut Rice**, either white or brown, use ¾ cup coconut milk (you can freeze the rest of the can for up to 6 months) and ½ cup water.

Sugar
Time!

Warm Salted Chocolate Chip Cookies

There are a zillion chocolate chip cookie recipes in the world, but this is THE One. You get the crisp and the chewy, you get the butterscotch-chocolaty, and you get a little flaky salt on top. Serve these lovelies warm, while the chocolate is still a little melty. The dough keeps in the fridge for up to five days, or in the freezer for three months, so you can take a little out at a time to have fresh-baked cookies whenever you want.

(See Weigh It Up, page 13.)

2 cups / 250 grams **all-purpose flour**

¾ teaspoon / 5 grams **kosher salt**

¾ teaspoon / 4 grams **baking powder**

½ teaspoon / 3 grams **baking soda**

10 tablespoons / 1¼ sticks / 142 grams **unsalted butter**, at room temperature

½ cup / 100 grams **granulated sugar**

½ cup / 100 grams **light brown sugar**

3 tablespoons / 38 grams **dark brown sugar** (or use light brown sugar; see Tips & Tweaks, page 248)

1 large **egg**, at room temperature

1 tablespoon / 12 grams **vanilla extract**

9 ounces / 255 grams **chocolate chunks** or **chips** (about 1½ cups chips)

Flaky sea salt, such as Maldon, for sprinkling (see Tips & Tweaks, page 248)

get it set

Take the egg and butter out of the fridge 30 to 60 minutes ahead to let them come to room temperature. (See When Not to Be Chill, page 255.)

Heat the oven to 350°F if baking right away.

Line 2 large cookie sheets with parchment paper or silicone liners, or grease them lightly.

Fit an electric stand mixer with the paddle attachment, or take out a handheld mixer.

Set out all your other ingredients.

1. In a medium bowl, mix together the flour, salt, baking powder, and baking soda.

2. In a large bowl using the electric mixer, beat the butter on medium speed until creamy, 1 to 3 minutes. Add the sugars (granulated, light brown, and dark brown), then beat until fluffy, about 2 minutes. Beat in the egg until smooth. Beat in the vanilla.

(recipe continues)

3. On low speed, gradually beat in the flour mixture. Use a rubber spatula to scrape down the sides of the bowl, making sure everything is incorporated. If it isn't, beat it again for a few seconds. Briefly mix in the chocolate chunks. (If you're not baking these cookies right away, scrape the dough into a container and chill for up to 5 days.)

4. Use a 1½-inch cookie scoop or a tablespoon to scoop balls of dough onto the prepared sheets, spacing them 2 inches apart so the cookies can spread.

5. Sprinkle the cookies lightly with flaky salt. Bake until the edges turn golden brown, 10 to 15 minutes; the centers will still be soft but will firm up as they cool. Transfer the cookie sheets to wire racks to cool slightly. If possible, serve the cookies warm. Or store in an airtight container at room temperature for up to 1 week.

tips & tweaks

● You can form the chilled cookie dough into balls, put the balls in an airtight container or resealable plastic bag, and freeze them for up to 3 months. When it's time to bake, put the frozen balls on cookie sheets and bake as directed in Step 5, but add 2 to 3 minutes to the baking time.

● The combo of light and dark brown sugar gives a more caramelly cookie, but using all light brown is totally fine.

● Sprinkling the tops of the cookies with a flaky sea salt, like Maldon or another brand, is a pro move that really takes the cookies to the next level, making the chocolate and caramel flavors pop.

● Substitute M&M's or Reese's Pieces for the chocolate chunks. Or use half white chocolate chips and half bittersweet chocolate.

● Go nuts! Add ½ cup coarsely chopped toasted walnuts, pecans, cashews, almonds, peanuts, or hazelnuts . . . you name it.

● If you want to give these a healthier spin, substitute ½ cup whole-wheat or rye flour for an equal amount of all-purpose flour.

Shortcut Sugar Cookie Bars

Sweet, soft, and supremely buttery, these sugar cookies don't have to be rolled or cut into shapes. Just spread the batter onto a sheet pan, bake, then cut into bars. Frosting and decorations make these particularly dazzling. This is a quick, easy way to make a large batch of treats for a party or a picnic.

(See Weigh It Up, page 13.)

for the cookies

4 cups / 500 grams **all-purpose flour**

1 teaspoon / 6 grams **kosher salt**

1 teaspoon / 5 grams **baking powder**

1½ cups / 3 sticks / 340 grams **unsalted butter,** at room temperature

1¼ cups / 250 grams **granulated sugar**

2 large **eggs,** at room temperature

1 teaspoon **vanilla extract** or ¼ teaspoon **almond extract**

1 teaspoon grated **lemon zest** (optional)

for the icing

½ cup / 1 stick / 113 grams **unsalted butter,** at room temperature

2½ cups / 306 grams **confectioners' sugar**

1 tablespoon **milk** or **heavy cream,** plus more as needed

1 teaspoon **fresh lemon juice**

1 teaspoon **vanilla extract** or ¼ teaspoon almond extract

¼ teaspoon **fine sea salt**

A drop or two of **food coloring** (optional)

Assorted sprinkles, for decorating (optional)

get it set

Take the eggs and butter out of the fridge 30 to 60 minutes ahead to let them come to room temperature. (See When Not to Be Chill, page 255.)

Heat the oven to 350°F.

Lightly grease a rimmed 17 x 13-inch sheet pan.

Fit an electric stand mixer with the paddle attachment, or take out a handheld mixer.

Set out all your other ingredients.

1. In a large bowl, whisk together the flour, salt, and baking powder.

2. In the bowl of an electric mixer fitted with the paddle attachment, or in a large bowl using a handheld mixer, beat the butter and granulated sugar on medium speed until light and fluffy, about 2 minutes. Beat in the eggs, one at a time, until fully incorporated. Beat in the extract and zest if using.

3. Reduce mixer speed to low and gradually beat in the flour mixture. Scrape the sides of the bowl with a rubber spatula.

(recipe continues)

4. Spread the batter into the prepared pan. The easiest way to do it is to use a small offset spatula. It's a sticky batter, so go slowly and methodically. You are aiming to spread the batter in an even thickness, but it doesn't have to be perfect; icing hides all. Alternatively, you can press the batter into the pan using floured hands.

5. Bake until the cookies are pale golden brown all over the surface and darker brown at the edges, 17 to 27 minutes. (The darker the color, the more crisp the cookies.) Transfer the pan to a wire rack to cool completely.

6. To make the icing, in the bowl of an electric mixer fitted with the paddle attachment, or in a large bowl using a handheld mixer, beat the butter until creamy. Decrease the speed to low and add the confectioners' sugar, a little at a time, until the icing is smooth. Beat in the milk, lemon juice, extract, and salt, adding more milk if needed to make a creamy, spreadable icing. Add a drop or two of food coloring if you like.

7. Spread the icing over the cookies, then decorate with sprinkles if you like. Cut into bars for serving. The cookies will keep for up to 1 week stored airtight at room temperature.

classic sugar cookies

To make Classic Sugar Cookies: After making the dough, form it into 4 large disks, wrap them in plastic, and chill for at least 2 hours (or up to 3 days).

When ready to bake, heat oven to 350°F. Dust a work surface lightly with flour and, using a floured rolling pin, roll one disk of the dough at a time out to ⅛ inch thick (keep remaining dough refrigerated until needed).

Cut cookies out with cookie cutters, then transfer to parchment paper–lined (or greased) cookie sheets, spacing them an inch apart.

Bake until golden, 12 to 15 minutes. Cool completely on wire racks while still on the cookie sheets.

Use the frosting and sprinkles to decorate.

One-Bowl Shortbread, Almond Edition

MAKES 18 BARS

Shortbread is one of my favorite treats. I adore its crumbly, buttery texture, and I love tweaking it a million different ways. This version is almondy, but see Tips & Tweaks for other ideas. The cookies are great dunked in a bowl of sliced strawberries and whipped cream for a crunchier take on strawberry shortcake.

(See Weigh It Up, page 13.)

2 cups / 250 grams **all-purpose flour**

¼ cup / 24 grams **almond flour**

¼ cup / 50 grams **granulated sugar,** plus another 2 to 5 tablespoons for sprinkling

¾ teaspoon / 4 grams **fine sea salt**

1 cup / 2 sticks / 225 grams **unsalted butter,** melted and cooled

¼ teaspoon **almond extract**

get it set

Heat the oven to 350°F.

Line the bottom of an 8 x 8-inch baking pan with parchment paper, leaving two edges long so they overhang the pan by at least an inch on each side. (These become handles for lifting out the bars after baking.)

Set out all your ingredients.

1. In a large bowl, whisk together the all-purpose flour, almond flour, sugar, and salt. Stir in the butter and the almond extract, and mix until you have a smooth dough. You might have to knead it a little with your hands to incorporate all the flour, and this is okay.

2. Press the dough evenly into the prepared baking pan. Bake until the top is golden brown, 35 to 45 minutes.

3. Transfer the pan to a wire rack, and immediately sprinkle the hot shortbread evenly and generously with sugar (use at least another 2 to 4 tablespoons, depending on how sweet you like it). Let the shortbread cool for 10 minutes, then use a butter knife to slice it into rectangles in the pan while it is still warm. Let the shortbread cool completely in the pan before lifting it out, using the parchment as handles.

tips & tweaks

● You have to cut these into bars while they are still warm; otherwise they shatter under your knife and turn into a crumbly heap.

Vanilla Shortbread

Substitute rice flour or cornstarch for the almond flour and use 1 teaspoon vanilla extract in place of the almond extract.

Or use the seeds from 1 vanilla bean: Lay a vanilla bean on a cutting board and use a paring knife to split it in half lengthwise. Use the tip of the knife to scrape out the goopy seeds. Add that goop to the flour in the bowl. And save the scraped-out beans! Stick them in your sugar to give it a vanilla-y aroma.

Citrus Shortbread

Substitute rice flour or cornstarch for the almond flour, and use 1 teaspoon finely grated lemon, lime, or orange zest in place of the almond extract. If you like, add a few drops of citrus flavoring oils or extracts as well.

Coconut Shortbread

Substitute coconut flour or finely grated unsweetened coconut flakes for the almond flour and use 1 teaspoon coconut extract in place of the almond extract.

Cardamom Almond Shortbread

Add 1 teaspoon ground cardamom to the flour mixture along with the almond extract. Or substitute rosewater for the almond extract to make Cardamom Rose Shortbread.

Rosemary Shortbread

Substitute rice flour or cornstarch for the almond flour. Use 1 tablespoon finely chopped fresh rosemary leaves in place of the almond extract. To make rosemary-lemon shortbread, add ½ teaspoon finely grated lemon zest as well.

Chewy Butterscotch Oatmeal Cookies

Shockingly, there's no Scotch in butterscotch, and it doesn't even have to have butter in it (though it usually does). Butterscotch gets its flavor from loads of brown sugar. These chewy cookies have a little of everything: chewy sweetness from raisins, a nubby crunch from oatmeal, and a bit of zing from cinnamon and cardamom.

(See Weigh It Up, page 13.)

1 cup / 2 sticks / 227 grams **unsalted butter**, at room temperature

1½ cups / 300 grams packed **dark brown sugar**

2 large **eggs**, at room temperature

2 tablespoons / 25 grams **vanilla extract**

1½ cups / 190 grams **all-purpose flour**

¾ teaspoon / 4 grams **fine sea salt**

1 teaspoon / 5 grams **baking soda**

1 teaspoon / 4 grams **ground cinnamon**

¼ teaspoon **ground cardamom** or **ground ginger**

3 cups / 270 grams **old-fashioned rolled oats** (not instant)

1½ cups / 225 grams **raisins**

get it set

Take the eggs and butter out of the fridge 30 to 60 minutes ahead to let them come to room temperature. (See When Not to Be Chill, opposite page.)

Heat the oven to 350°F.

Line 4 large cookie sheets with parchment paper or silicone liners, or grease them lightly. (If you don't have 4 cookie sheets, work in batches.)

Fit an electric stand mixer with the paddle attachment, or take out a handheld mixer.

Set out all your other ingredients.

1. In a large bowl, using the mixer, beat the butter on medium speed until creamy, 1 to 3 minutes (the softer the butter is, the faster this goes). Add the brown sugar and beat until fluffy, about 2 minutes. Beat in the eggs, one at a time. Beat in the vanilla extract.

2. In a medium bowl, mix together the flour, salt, baking soda, cinnamon, and cardamom. On low speed, gradually beat the flour mixture into the butter-sugar mixture. Then beat in the oats. Use a rubber spatula to scrape down the sides of the bowl, making sure everything is incorporated. If it isn't, beat it again for a few seconds. Finally, beat in the raisins.

3. Use a 1½-inch cookie scoop or a tablespoon to scoop balls of the dough onto the prepared cookie sheets, spacing them about 2 inches apart so the cookies have room to spread.

4. Bake until the edges of the cookies turn golden brown, 11 to 15 minutes; the centers will still be quite soft but will firm up as the cookies cool. Transfer the cookie sheets to wire racks to cool. Store the cookies in an airtight container at room temperature.

when not to be chill

Ingredients in baking don't combine well unless they're at the same temperature. That's why we bring things like eggs and butter to room temperature before combining them: because otherwise you'll get butter clumps or egg white pockets in your batter.

But don't stress if your ingredients are still too chill! Here are the cheat codes:

Eggs fresh from the fridge can be placed, in their shells, in a bowl of warm (not hot) water for 10 minutes.

Cold butter can be softened by placing it in a bowl and microwaving it at 50% power for 20 seconds to a minute. Check it every 10 seconds and pull it out before it melts. We're looking for softened, not liquid.

tips & tweaks

● You can make the cookie dough up to 3 days ahead and store it in the fridge. Using cold cookie dough will actually give you neater and more uniform-looking cookies if you form the dough into balls before putting them on the cookie sheet. The dough is too sticky to do this when it's at room temperature.

● Not a raisin fan? Leave them out, or substitute the same amount of dried cherries or other chopped dried fruit, chopped candied ginger, or shredded coconut (either sweetened or unsweetened). Or use chocolate chips or chocolate chunks for the best of both cookie worlds.

● Turn these into granola cookies by substituting 1 cup of granola for ½ cup raisins and ½ cup oats.

Gingery Peanut Butter Cookies

Chewy bits of candied ginger add a spicy jolt to these classic and very dunkable peanut butter cookies. They are crunchy and crumbly and will keep for at least a week–unless you eat them all first. Which is highly likely, especially if you slather Nutella between them to make a cookie sandwich.

(See Weigh It Up, page 13.)

1½ cups / 190 grams **all-purpose flour**

1 teaspoon / 5 grams **baking soda**

¼ teaspoon **fine sea salt**

8 tablespoons / 1 stick / 113 grams **unsalted butter**, at room temperature

¾ cup / 180 grams salted natural **peanut butter**, smooth or chunky

1 cup / 200 grams packed **dark brown sugar**

1 large **egg**, at room temperature

1 tablespoon / 12 grams **vanilla extract**

½ cup / 115 grams chopped **candied ginger**

3 tablespoons / 38 grams **Demerara sugar** or **turbinado sugar** (or use granulated sugar)

get it set

Take the egg and butter out of the fridge 30 to 60 minutes ahead to let them come to room temperature. (See When Not to Be Chill, page 255.)

Heat the oven to 350°F.

Line 3 large cookie sheets with parchment paper or silicone liners, or grease them lightly. (If you don't have 3 cookie sheets, work in batches.)

Fit an electric stand mixer with the paddle attachment, or take out a handheld mixer.

Set out all your other ingredients.

1. In a large bowl, whisk together the flour, baking soda, and salt.

2. Using an electric mixer, in a large bowl, beat together the butter, peanut butter, and brown sugar together on medium speed until light and creamy, 2 to 3 minutes. Beat in the egg and vanilla until well combined.

3. With the mixer on low speed, gradually beat in the flour mixture until combined. Scrape down the sides of the bowl with a rubber spatula to make sure everything is incorporated. If it isn't, beat again for another few seconds. Then beat in the candied ginger.

4. Use a 1½-inch cookie scoop or a tablespoon to scoop balls of dough onto the prepared cookie sheets, spacing them about 1½ inches apart so the cookies have room to spread. Use a fork to gently press a crisscross pattern on top of each cookie, flattening the balls only slightly.

5. Sprinkle the cookies evenly with the Demerara or turbinado sugar (this coarse sugar stays nice and crunchy after baking). Bake until they're light brown on the edges, 12 to 17 minutes. Remove from the oven and let the cookies cool on the cookie sheets for 5 minutes. Then use a metal spatula to transfer the cookies to wire racks to cool completely.

tips & tweaks

● You can make the cookie dough up to 3 days ahead and store it in the fridge.

mighty morphin' peanut butter cookies

Leave it out!	Put it in!
candied ginger	*The same amount of one of these:* ● raisins ● dried cherries ● chopped apricots ● chocolate chips ● white chocolate chips ● chopped roasted peanuts
peanut butter	*The same amount of one of these:* ● almond butter ● cashew butter ● sunflower butter

Deep Dark Fudgy Brownies

A combination of butter and oil makes these the fudgiest brownies known to dessert science—the butter adds flavor and the oil keeps everything moist. Brownies like these are so distractingly good, they could easily be used to take over the world. I'm giving you the Level 1 chocolate version, which has a little sea salt on top to make the chocolate flavor pop. But feel free to tweak it up as much as you like. The peppermint candy versions are my personal favorites.

(See Weigh It Up, page 13.)

2 ounces **unsweetened chocolate,** coarsely chopped or broken up

5 tablespoons / 70 grams **unsalted butter**

⅓ cup **sunflower oil** or other neutral oil (grapeseed, canola, or even a mild olive oil will work)

1½ cups / 300 grams **sugar**

1 cup / 125 grams **all-purpose flour**

¼ cup / 25 grams **unsweetened cocoa powder** (see Cocoa Two Ways, page 260)

¾ teaspoon / 4 grams **kosher salt**

2 large **eggs**, at room temperature

2 teaspoons **vanilla extract**

⅓ cup **mini** or **regular chocolate chips**

Flaky sea salt, such as Maldon, for sprinkling

get it set

Take the eggs out of the fridge 30 to 60 minutes ahead so they can come to room temperature. (See When Not to Be Chill, page 255.)

Heat the oven to 350°F.

Lightly grease an 8 x 8-inch baking pan.

Set out all your other ingredients.

1. Put the chocolate and the butter in a small saucepan and place it over low heat. Let them melt, stirring the mixture frequently, until smooth.

2. Using a rubber spatula, scrape the chocolate mixture into a large bowl. Whisk in the oil and the sugar and let it cool for about 5 minutes.

3. While the chocolate mixture is cooling, in a medium bowl, whisk together the flour, cocoa powder, and kosher salt.

(recipe continues)

4. Crack the eggs into the cooled chocolate mixture and whisk well. Whisk in the vanilla. (The mixture may look curdled and that is normal.) Add the flour mixture to the bowl and use a rubber spatula to fold it in until just combined. Fold in the chocolate chips.

5. Scrape the batter into the prepared baking pan and smooth it into an even layer. Sprinkle the top lightly with flaky sea salt. Bake until the top is firm and set, 17 to 23 minutes. If you test it with a toothpick, it will seem wet. That's okay. It solidifies as it cools. Don't overbake these. Underbaked and runny is better than dry.

6. Transfer the pan to a wire rack and let it cool for at least 1½ hours before cutting into 16 brownies.

cocoa two ways

There are two kinds of unsweetened cocoa powder: natural, and Dutch process. Natural cocoa powder (made from ground cocoa beans) has a slightly more intense flavor that's also a bit acidic. "Dutch process" means the beans have been treated with an alkaline solution (potassium carbonate) in order to neutralize their acid, a process that softens their flavor and deepens their color, giving the powder a reddish tinge. For this recipe you can use either one. The natural powder will be a little more intense tasting, the Dutch process darker in color and smoother in taste. The difference is noticeable but subtle.

tips & tweaks

● There are endless add-in possibilities for brownies. Mix in about ⅓ cup:

- Chopped toasted nuts
- Shredded coconut
- Raisins or dried cherries
- Rice Krispies or a similar cereal
- White chocolate chips or butterscotch chips
- Reese's Pieces or M&M's
- Chopped-up Peppermint Patties or peanut butter cups

● Or try sprinkling ⅓ cup smashed candy canes or hard peppermint candies on top before baking: Put the candy in a clean dish towel, put the dish towel in a plastic bag, and whack it with a rolling pin until the candies are crushed but not powdery. You want some texture.

Think Pink Lemonade Bars

If you love lemon squares and you enjoy (or at least tolerate) the color pink, you'll flip for these fruity, tangy bars. They've got a crunchy shortbread crust (which is a bona fide cookie all on its own, so two-for-one!), plus a rosy, tart-sweet topping that's pretty *and* tasty. Or go with the purple version in Tips & Tweaks. There's room for everyone.

(See Weigh It Up, page 13.)

for the crust

1½ cups / 190 grams **all-purpose flour**

⅓ cup / 66 grams **granulated sugar**

¼ teaspoon **kosher sea salt**

12 tablespoons / 1½ sticks / 170 grams cold **unsalted butter**, cut into 1-inch pieces

for the filling

½ cup sliced **strawberries**

4 large **eggs**, at room temperature

1 cup / 200 grams **granulated sugar**

½ cup **fresh lemon juice** (from 2 to 3 lemons)

3 tablespoons / 25 grams **all-purpose flour**

1 tablespoon finely grated **lemon zest**

Pinch of **fine sea salt**

Confectioners' sugar, for serving

get it set

Take the eggs out of the fridge 30 to 60 minutes ahead so they can come to room temperature. (See When Not to Be Chill, page 255.)

Heat the oven to 325°F.

Line a 9 x 9-inch baking pan with parchment paper, leaving two edges long so they overhang the pan by at least an inch on each side. (These become handles for lifting the bars out after baking.)

Set out all your other ingredients.

1. Make the crust: In a food processor, pulse together the flour, granulated sugar, and salt. Add the butter and process until a crumbly dough forms, about 30 seconds. Dump the crumbs into the prepared baking pan and use your hands to press them into an even layer. (Shake out the food processor bowl, but you don't have to wash it.)

2. Bake the crust until it's golden around the edges, 35 to 40 minutes.

(recipe continues)

3. While the crust is baking, **make the filling:** In the same food processor bowl, combine the strawberries, eggs, granulated sugar, lemon juice, flour, lemon zest, and salt. Process everything until it's pureed, 1 to 2 minutes. Leave the mixture in the food processor bowl until the crust is ready.

4. Remove the baked crust from the oven and raise the oven temperature to 350°F.

5. As soon as the crust is done baking, give the topping mixture another pulse or two to mix it up again, and pour it into the hot baked crust. Return the pan to the oven and bake until the topping is just firm and set, 15 to 20 minutes. Transfer the baking pan to a wire rack and let it cool completely.

6. Once it is cool, run a butter knife around the inside edges of the pan to free up the crust. Lift the pastry out of the pan, using the parchment handles, and place it on a cutting board. Use a sharp knife to cut it into bars. Dust them with confectioners' sugar before serving.

tips & tweaks

● Turn these into Pink Limeade Bars by substituting lime juice and zest for the lemon. If you like sour, this one's for you!

● Turn these purplish by substituting blueberries for the strawberries. This tastes especially great with the limeade version, and, well, it's *purple*.

It's Your Birthday, Ep. 1:
Impressive Golden Cake with Fudge Frosting

MAKES ONE 8- OR 9-INCH LAYER CAKE, SERVING 8 TO 12

A soft golden cake slathered in a fudgy chocolate frosting, this classic three-layer beauty is *the* thing to make for birthday (and all other) celebrations. (That is, unless you like the next recipe more.) And you can customize it, adding different flavors or switching up the icing or making it a Funfetti cake (see Tips & Tweaks).

(See Weigh It Up, page 13.)

Nonstick cooking spray, preferably coconut oil spray

for the cake

3 cups / 375 grams **all-purpose flour,** plus more for the pans

2½ teaspoons / 12 grams **baking powder**

½ teaspoon / 3 grams **fine sea salt**

2 cups / 400 grams **granulated sugar**

1 cup / 2 sticks / 225 grams **unsalted butter,** at room temperature

3 large **eggs,** at room temperature

1 large **egg yolk,** at room temperature

1 tablespoon / 12 grams **vanilla extract**

1 cup / 240 grams **whole milk,** at room temperature

for the frosting

1½ cups / 3 sticks / 338 grams **unsalted butter,** at room temperature, divided

9 ounces / 255 grams **bittersweet chocolate,** chopped

Pinch of **fine sea salt**

2½ cups / 310 grams **confectioners' sugar**

1 tablespoon / 15 grams **whole milk**

1 teaspoon / 4 grams **vanilla extract**

get it set

Heat the oven to 350°F.

Take the butter, eggs, and milk out of the fridge 30 to 60 minutes ahead to allow them to come to room temperature. (See When Not to Be Chill, page 255.)

Butter or spray three 8- or 9-inch cake pans with nonstick cooking spray. (If you don't have 3 pans, you can bake the cake layers in batches.)

Fit an electric stand mixer with the paddle attachment, and have the whisk attachment at the ready. Or get out a handheld electric mixer.

Other special equipment: Offset metal spatula (or a butter knife will work)

Set out all your other ingredients.

1. Make the cake layers: In a medium bowl, whisk together the flour, baking powder, and salt.

(recipe continues)

2. Using an electric mixer, in a large bowl, beat together the granulated sugar and butter on medium speed until light and fluffy, about 3 minutes. One by one, add the whole eggs and the yolk, beating between additions for each egg to fully combine with the butter. Beat in the vanilla. Then scrape down the sides of the bowl with a rubber spatula to make sure everything is incorporated (if it isn't, beat the mixture again).

3. Reduce the mixer speed to low and gradually add the milk (if you add the milk all at once, it will splash up out of the bowl in a messy wet wave). Scrape down the bowl again. Then gradually add the flour mixture and beat just to combine.

4. Divide the batter evenly among the prepared cake pans, and smooth the tops. Bake for 15 minutes. Then, wearing oven mitts, rotate the pans 180 degrees so the cakes bake evenly. Continue to bake until the cakes are golden and the tops spring back when lightly pressed in the center, another 10 to 15 minutes (for a total baking time of 25 to 30 minutes). A tester inserted in the center of the cake should emerge either clean or with a few crumbs sticking to it, but it shouldn't be wet.

5. Transfer the cakes to a wire rack and let them cool completely in their pans. To unmold the cooled cake layers, run a butter knife or a thin metal spatula around the inner edge of the pans and then invert them onto the wire rack.

6. When you are ready to assemble the cake, **make the frosting:** In a large microwave-safe bowl, combine 1 cup (2 sticks) of the butter with the chocolate and the salt. Microwave in 30-second intervals, stirring after each one. (Or you can do this in a small pot over low heat on the stove.) Once the mixture is melted and smooth, cut the remaining ½ cup of butter into cubes and stir them into the hot chocolate mixture. Let it sit for a minute, then stir everything together (the heat from the chocolate should melt this last stick of butter, and adding the room-temperature butter at this point helps cool down the mixture).

7. Transfer the chocolate mixture to the bowl of an electric stand mixer fitted with the whisk (or use a handheld electric mixer with clean beaters), and add the confectioners' sugar. Beat on low speed until combined, then beat in the milk and vanilla. Raise the speed to high and beat until the mixture is thick and fluffy, about 5 minutes. If it's still soft, stick the frosting in the fridge for 20 minutes, then beat it again to fluff it up.

8. To assemble and ice the layers, see How to Frost a Cake (page 268).

---

tips & tweaks

● You can bake the cake layers, let them cool, and unmold them the day before you plan to serve the cake.

Wrap them in plastic wrap and store them in the refrigerator. The frosting is best made just before assembling the cake; otherwise it may get grainy. The cake can be assembled up to 8 hours before serving and kept at a cool room temperature; if your kitchen is hot, stick it in the fridge.

● To make cupcakes: Fill 24 cupcake molds (set with paper liners) three-fourths full; bake for 20 to 25 minutes.

● To make a sheet cake: Scrape the batter into a greased 9 x 13-inch cake pan. Bake for 30 to 40 minutes.

● Swap the cream cheese frosting (on page 270) for chocolate fudge frosting.

● Turn this into a Funfetti cake: Fold in ½ cup rainbow sprinkles right before you transfer the batter to the cake pans. Then use more sprinkles to decorate the frosted cake.

● Don't want plain ol' vanilla? Change the cake flavor! Try one of these:

• **Citrus:** Instead of the vanilla extract, add 1½ tablespoons finely grated lemon, lime, or orange zest to the dry ingredients in Step 1.

• **Almond:** Reduce the vanilla extract in the cake to ½ tablespoon and add 1 teaspoon almond extract. You can also swap out ¾ cup all-purpose flour for blanched almond flour.

• **Coconut:** Reduce the vanilla extract in the cake to ½ tablespoon and add 1 tablespoon coconut extract. Top the cake with toasted coconut flakes if you like.

how to frost a cake

I strongly suggest checking out one of the many instructive cake frosting how-to videos online. Seeing the process really helps!

Here's what to do:

1. Place four 2-inch-wide strips of parchment paper on the outer rim of a serving platter to protect it from getting covered in frosting.

2. Brush any loose crumbs from the thoroughly cooled cake layers and place one layer upside down (domed-side down) on the platter on top of the strips (they should stick out to cover the plate around the cake).

3. Using an offset spatula or a butter knife, spread ¾ cup of the frosting over the top of the layer, leaving a ½-inch border.

4. Top the first layer with another cake layer, domed-side down. Frost that layer the same way. Then top it with the final layer, domed-side up.

5. Starting with the sides, spread a very thin layer of frosting all over the cake to seal in the crumbs (this is called a crumb coat). If you get any crumbs in the frosting bowl, use a spoon to scoop them out.

6. Now use the remaining frosting to cover the top and sides of the cake, swirling it decoratively if you like. Pull the parchment strips out from under the cake. Done!

It's Your Birthday, Ep. 2:
Chocolate Cake with
Fluffy Cream Cheese Frosting

MAKES ONE 8- OR 9-INCH CAKE, SERVING 8 TO 12

This is the evil twin of the golden cake with fudge frosting: It has a devil's-food heart beneath icing as fluffy and white as a kitten. Or to be completely and unapologetically chocolaty, use the fudge frosting on page 265. Sorry not sorry.

(See Weigh It Up, page 13.)

for the cake

2 cups / 250 grams **all-purpose flour,** plus more for the pans

1 cup / 85 grams **Dutch-process unsweetened cocoa powder** (see Cocoa Two Ways, page 260)

2½ teaspoons / 12 grams **baking powder**

½ teaspoon / 3 grams **fine sea salt**

1 cup plus 2 tablespoons / 2¼ sticks / 240 grams **unsalted butter,** at room temperature

2 cups / 400 grams **granulated sugar**

3 large **eggs,** at room temperature

1 tablespoon / 12 grams **vanilla extract**

¾ cup / 184 grams **whole milk,** at room temperature

for the frosting

1 cup / 2 sticks / 225 grams **unsalted butter,** at room temperature

16 ounces (2 bricks) **cream cheese,** cut into chunks, at room temperature

2½ cups / 310 grams **confectioners' sugar**

2 tablespoons / 30 grams **whole milk**

2 teaspoons / 8 grams **vanilla extract**

get it set

Heat the oven to 350°F.

Take the butter, eggs, milk, and cream cheese out of the fridge 30 to 60 minutes ahead to allow them to come to room temperature. (See When Not to Be Chill, page 255.)

Butter or spray three 8- or 9-inch cake pans with nonstick cooking spray.

Fit an electric stand mixer with the paddle attachment or get out a handheld electric mixer.

Other special equipment: Offset metal spatula (or butter knife will work)

Set out all your other ingredients.

1. Make the cake: In a medium bowl, whisk together the flour, cocoa powder, baking powder, and salt.

2. Using an electric mixer, in a large bowl, beat together the butter and granulated sugar on medium speed until light and fluffy, about 3 minutes. One by one, add the eggs, beating between additions. Beat in the vanilla, then scrape down the sides of the bowl with a rubber spatula to make sure everything is incorporated.

3. Reduce the mixer speed to low and gradually add the milk. Scrape down the bowl again, then gradually add the flour mixture and beat just to combine.

4. Divide the batter evenly among the prepared cake pans, and smooth the tops. Bake for 10 minutes. Then, wearing oven mitts, rotate the pans 180 degrees so the cakes bake evenly. Continue to bake until the cakes are risen and firm and the tops spring back when lightly pressed in the center, another 10 to 18 minutes (for a total baking time of 20 to 28 minutes). A tester inserted in the center of the cake should emerge either clean or with a few crumbs sticking to it, but it shouldn't be wet.

5. Transfer the cakes to a wire rack and let them cool completely in their pans. To unmold the cooled cake layers, run a butter knife or a thin metal spatula around the inner edge of each pan to release the cake, then invert them onto the wire rack.

6. When you are ready to assemble the cake, **make the frosting:** Put the butter in a bowl and, using an electric mixer fitted with the whisk (or beaters), beat until it is fluffy, about 1 minute. Add the chunks of cream cheese and beat until smooth, 1 to 3 minutes (this will happen more quickly if the butter and cream cheese are really soft). Gradually add the confectioners' sugar, beating on low speed. Beat in the milk and vanilla. Raise the speed to high and beat until the mixture is thick and fluffy, about 5 minutes. If it's still soft, chill it for 20 minutes, then beat it again to fluff it up.

7. To assemble and ice the layers, see How to Frost a Cake (page 268).

---

tips & tweaks

● You can bake, cool, and unmold the cake layers the day before serving. Wrap them in plastic wrap and store them in the refrigerator. The frosting is best made just before assembling the cake; otherwise it could get grainy. The cake can be assembled up to 8 hours before serving and kept at a cool room temperature; if your kitchen is hot, the finished cake is better off in the fridge.

● To make cupcakes or a sheet cake, see Tips & Tweaks, page 267.

● Instead of the vanilla in the cake, start with ¼ teaspoon almond, coconut, or peppermint extract and beat in more, a drop at a time, to taste. These extracts are a lot more intense than vanilla, so you'll need less.

• **Citrus:** Beat in 1 tablespoon finely grated lemon, lime, or orange zest after you add the butter and sugar in Step 2.

• **Spices:** Beat in 1 teaspoon ground ginger, cinnamon, or cardamom after you add the butter and sugar in Step 2.

Gingerbread Snack Cake

Moist and molasses-y, this highly spiced cake tastes like Christmas but is the perfect snack for any day of the year. You don't need a mixer to make it—just a whisk and a bowl (well, and a baking pan, clearly). With a little confectioners' sugar or lemony glaze to gussy it up (see sidebar, opposite), it's an ideal after-school bite.

(See Weigh It Up, page 13.)

2 cups / 250 grams **all-purpose flour**

1½ teaspoons / 8 grams **baking powder**

1 tablespoon / 10 grams **ground ginger**

1 teaspoon / 4 grams **ground cinnamon**

½ teaspoon / 3 grams **baking soda**

¼ teaspoon **ground cloves**

¼ teaspoon **fine sea salt**

3 large **eggs**, at room temperature

1 cup / 200 grams **dark brown sugar**

¾ cup **neutral oil**, such as sunflower, grapeseed, or canola

½ cup / 100 grams **granulated sugar**

1 cup / 240 grams **whole milk**

1 cup / 320 grams **light unsulfured molasses**

Confectioners' sugar, for serving

get it set

Take the eggs out of the fridge 30 to 60 minutes ahead so they can come to room temperature. (See When Not to Be Chill, page 255.)

Heat the oven to 350°F.

Grease a 9 x 9-inch baking pan and line it with parchment paper, leaving two edges long so they overhang the pan by at least an inch on each side. (These become handles for lifting the cake out after baking.)

Set out all your other ingredients.

1. In a medium bowl, whisk together the flour, baking powder, ginger, cinnamon, baking soda, cloves, and sea salt.

2. In a large bowl, whisk together the eggs, brown sugar, oil, and granulated sugar. Add the milk and molasses and whisk until smooth. Whisk in the flour mixture, whisking vigorously to eliminate any lumps.

3. Scrape the batter into the prepared baking pan. Bake until the top bounces back when lightly pressed and the edges of the cake are starting to pull away from the pan, 70 to 80 minutes. A tester inserted into the center of the cake should come out with a few crumbs attached. Transfer the pan to a wire rack and let it cool completely.

4. To serve, run a butter knife around the inside edges of the pan to release the cooled cake, then lift out the cake using the parchment handles. Peel off the paper and put the cake on a cutting board or serving dish. Sprinkle the top with confectioners' sugar or pour Simple Lemon Glaze over top. Cut it into squares for serving.

simple lemon glaze

Add a tangy sweetness to gingerbread with this easy lemon topping.

1 cup confectioners' sugar

1 tablespoon fresh lemon juice, plus more as needed

1 teaspoon finely grated lemon zest (optional)

1. In a small bowl, whisk together the confectioners' sugar and lemon juice. If the mixture is too thick to pour, add a few more drops of lemon juice, whisking until the glaze is thick but pourable.

2. Pour the glaze over the cake after you've taken it out of the pan. Scatter the lemon zest all over the top of the glaze if you like. Let set for at least 1 hour before serving.

Summer Fruit Galette

A fruit galette is a free-form crust folded around a fruit filling. That's right—it's pie! But it's pie with half the work and just as much satisfaction. It's also one of those "I woke up this way" pastries that looks great *because* of its imperfections, which are gorgeously golden. The sweet, ripe summer fruit is bursting with flavor and works great when served à la mode, so pile it on!

(See Weigh It Up, page 13.)

for the dough

- 1 large **egg**, at room temperature
- 1 to 3 tablespoons **heavy cream**, plus more for brushing the crust, at room temperature
- 1⅓ cups / 165 grams **all-purpose flour**, plus more for the work surface
- 1 tablespoon / 15 grams **granulated sugar**
- ½ teaspoon / 3 grams **fine sea salt**
- ½ cup / 1 stick / 113 grams **unsalted butter**, very cold, cut into big cubes

for the filling

- 1 small **lemon**
- 3 cups **summer fruit** (see Tips & Tweaks), sliced or cubed if necessary
- ½ to ¾ cup / 100 to 150 grams plus 1 tablespoon **granulated sugar**, divided
- Pinch of **fine sea salt**
- 3½ tablespoons / 30 grams **cornstarch**

get it set

Take the egg and cream out of the fridge 30 to 60 minutes ahead to let them come to room temperature. (See When Not to Be Chill, page 255.)

Other special equipment: Food processor (or you can use a bowl), rolling pin, pastry brush

Make sure you have a rimmed sheet pan.

Set out all your other ingredients.

1. **Make the dough:** Crack the egg into a measuring cup and beat it with a fork. Add enough heavy cream to measure ⅓ cup.

(recipe continues)

food processor

by hand

2. To make the crust in a food processor, combine the flour, sugar, and salt in the work bowl and pulse two or three times to combine. Add the cubed butter and pulse until the flour has formed jelly bean–size pieces (about ½ inch). Drizzle in the cream-egg mixture and pulse just to combine, taking care not overprocess the dough.

2. To make the dough by hand, put the flour, sugar, and salt in a large bowl and whisk to combine. Add the cubed butter and mix it in with your hands, pinching and squeezing the butter cubes with your fingers (or use a pastry blender) until the largest pieces are the size of M&M's (you want them smaller than if you were making this in the food processor). Drizzle in the cream-egg mixture a little at a time, mixing until the dough starts to come together.

3. Dump the dough onto a lightly floured work surface and squeeze and press it until it forms a ball. Flatten the dough into a disk, wrap it in plastic wrap, and refrigerate it for at least 2 hours or up to 3 days.

4. When you are ready to bake the galette, heat the oven to 400°F.

5. Place a piece of parchment paper on a work surface. Unwrap the dough and place it in the center of the parchment. Top it with another piece of paper. Using a rolling pin, roll the dough out to form a 12-inch round (it can be ragged). If the dough is too hard to roll, let it sit at room temperature for 5 to 10 minutes to soften slightly (but don't let it get too soft or it gets too sticky to roll; you're looking for cold but still roll-able). Leaving the dough sandwiched between the parchment, transfer it to a rimmed sheet pan (if it's not rimmed, the fruit juices may leak all over your oven–not good). Put the sheet pan in the fridge while you prepare the filling.

6. **Make the filling:** Using a Microplane grater or other fine grater, grate ½ teaspoon zest from the lemon and put it in a large bowl. Cut the lemon in half and squeeze one half into the bowl (spoon out any seeds).

7. Add the fruit to the bowl along with ½ cup of the sugar and the pinch of salt, and toss gently to combine. Taste a piece of fruit. If it seems sour, add more sugar. It should be balanced between sweet and tart. Add the cornstarch and toss gently.

8. Take the sheet pan out of the fridge and peel off the top piece of parchment. Pile the fruit on the dough, leaving a 1½-inch border. Gently fold the border up to hold the fruit (sloppy is totally fine). Brush the dough with more cream. Sprinkle the 1 tablespoon sugar on top.

9. Bake the tart for 30 to 45 minutes, until the crust is brown and the fruit is tender and the juices are actively bubbling (which means the filling is thickening; see Tips & Tweaks). Transfer the sheet pan to a wire rack and let it cool for at least 20 minutes before serving the galette straight from the pan.

You can use pretty much any summer stone fruit or berries here, but there are also a lot of fruits that don't work well in galettes:

very galettable	not galettable
● nectarines	**TOO WATERY:**
● peaches	● citrus
● apricots	● melons
● plums	● kiwi
● raspberries	
● blueberries	**WOULD REQUIRE INCONVENIENT PRECOOKING:**
● blackberries	● apples
● strawberries	● pineapple
● fresh figs	● grapes
● or a combination of any of the above	**TOO SOUR, AND TECHNICALLY A VEGETABLE ANYWAY:**
	● rhubarb

tips & tweaks

● It's important to see active bubbling in the filling before you take the tart out of the oven. A steady bubbling means that fruit juices are reacting with the cornstarch, which is what thickens the filling. One or two languid, lazy bubbles won't do it, so be patient and wait for the frenzy.

● You can substitute any pie dough here, including store-bought pie dough or puff pastry.

● Give your galette even more crunch by adding sliced almonds or finely chopped pistachios, walnuts, pecans, or hazelnuts. Sprinkle ¼ cup on top of the fruit before folding up the edges of the crust.

● Add jam to intensify the fruit flavors: Spread the bottom of the crust with about 2 tablespoons any flavor jam before adding the filling. This also makes it sweeter if your fruit isn't quite ripe, though it could be too sweet if it is.

Cozy Coconut Rice Pudding

SERVES 6 TO 8

Coconut fans will go cuckoo for this simple dessert. It's soft and creamy with a just-right sweetness, capped with toasted coconut flakes for a crazy-crisp crunch.

(See Weigh It Up, page 13.)

2½ cups / 590 mL / 613 grams **whole milk** (or nondairy milk)

1 (14-ounce) can **coconut milk** (don't use light coconut milk), divided

⅔ cup / 130 grams **short-grain white rice**, such as Arborio or sushi rice

⅓ cup / 66 grams **sugar**

Pinch of **fine sea salt**

2 large **egg yolks** (see How to Separate Eggs, page 37)

2 teaspoons **vanilla extract**

⅔ cup / 50 grams **sweetened coconut flakes**

Ground cinnamon, for serving

get it set

Set out all your ingredients.

1. In a medium pot over high heat, stir together the milk, 1¼ cups of the coconut milk, and the rice, sugar, and salt. Bring the mixture to a simmer, about 5 minutes.

2. Reduce the heat to medium-low and let the rice cook, uncovered, until it's very soft and the mixture has thickened, 35 to 45 minutes. Stir the rice every 5 to 10 minutes so it doesn't stick and burn (you can set a second timer if you want a reminder). While the rice is cooking, work on the next steps.

3. In a medium bowl, whisk the remaining ½ cup coconut milk with the egg yolks and vanilla. Set aside.

4. Make the topping: Heat a medium skillet over medium heat. Add the coconut flakes and cook, stirring often, until they're light brown and you can smell their toasty aroma, 2 to 5 minutes. Scrape the coconut flakes onto a plate to cool (this stops the cooking, so they won't get too dark and bitter).

5. Once the rice is done, remove the pot from the heat and stir the egg mixture into the hot pudding (the heat will cook the yolks, so do this as soon as your rice is done cooking).

6. You can serve the rice pudding either warm or cold. When warm, it's soft and runny; after cooling, it firms up and turns more pudding-like. Scoop it into serving bowls and top each serving with some toasted coconut and a sprinkle of cinnamon.

tips & tweaks

● Top the pudding with coconut right when you serve it. If you do this too early, the flakes can get soggy. It's tasty either way, but the crunch makes it better.

● Stir raisins, dried cherries, or other chopped dried fruit into the pudding when it's still warm.

Pick a Fruit, Any Fruit Popsicles

MAKES ABOUT 1½ CUPS POPSICLE BASE (ABOUT 6 STANDARD POPS, DEPENDING ON YOUR MOLDS)

Cool and fruity on a hot day, homemade pops are a breeze to make. This recipe is basically a MadLib where you fill in any fruit you like. All fruits are a go. Frozen fruit works, too, and you don't even have to thaw it first—just toss it in the blender and you're on your way.

1 cup **sugar**

1½ cups any **chopped fruit** or **berries** or a combination (see Tips & Tweaks)

½ cup chopped unpeeled **apple** or **pear** (optional; see Tips & Tweaks), or use more of the main fruit

1 to 2 tablespoons **fresh lemon juice**

get it set

SPECIAL EQUIPMENT: Blender, Popsicle molds or 2 ice cube trays

Put a small heatproof container with a lid, such as a mason jar or a jam jar, next to the stove.

Set out all your ingredients.

1. First, make the simple syrup: Combine the sugar with ½ cup water in a small pot and set it over medium-high heat. Bring to a boil, stirring once or twice, then reduce the heat and let simmer until the sugar dissolves, about 5 minutes. Carefully pour the syrup into a heatproof container, and let it cool (you can stick it in the fridge to speed the cooling along).

2. Meanwhile, put all the fruit and 1 tablespoon of the lemon juice in a blender and puree until very smooth. If you're using a fruit with seeds, such as blackberries or raspberries, you can either push the puree through a strainer or not, depending on your feelings about seeds.

(recipe continues)

3. Stir in simple syrup to taste, a little at a time (you definitely won't use it all). If the mixture tastes flat, add the rest of the lemon juice. The idea here is to balance the sweetness and tartness with simple syrup and lemon juice, adding both to taste as you go. You want the puree to end up slightly sweeter than you'd like the pop to be, because the sweetness will mellow once it's frozen.

4. Pour the mixture into Popsicle molds and freeze them for at least 3 hours, but preferably overnight. Or, if you don't have Popsicle molds, pour the mixture into ice cube trays and put them in the freezer; after about 30 minutes, stick toothpicks into the center of the partially frozen juice (if it's not solid enough yet, try again in 15 minutes). Freeze until solid, at least 3 hours or overnight.

tips & tweaks

● Simple syrup is sugar cooked in water until it melts. It's great to use in cold or uncooked recipes where granulated sugar wouldn't dissolve on its own and might leave a sandy texture. Simple syrup is also perfect for sweetening iced beverages like lemonade and iced tea. Leftover simple syrup will keep for at least a month in the fridge.

● If you have any fruit puree left over, save it in the fridge and stir it into seltzer.

● Use any variety or combination of fruit you want. Adding a little apple or pear, fruits that are high in pectin but mild in flavor, helps give Popsicles a creamy texture without adding much flavor. But you can leave them out and use other fruit instead; you'll need 2 cups of fruit total. If you're using only very watery fruit like citrus, watermelon, or cantaloupe, your Popsicles may become icy. But that's not always a bad thing in a pop.

● To make creamsicles, use 1½ cups orange juice and ½ cup half-and-half or whole milk in place of the fruit.

● Herb it up! Just throw a few fresh herb sprigs or leaves into the hot just-cooked syrup and let them cool with the mixture. Then strain or pluck out the herbs. Just stay away from chives, which are too savory to use here.

● Some of my favorite combos:
- **Pineapple + sage**
- **Peaches + basil**
- **Blackberry or blueberry + thyme**
- **Strawberry + mint**

Heartfelt thanks to everyone who helped cook up this book:

My parents, Julian and Rita Clark, taught me to dream big when I was the kid in a kitchen.

Star recipe developer Jade Zimmerman collaborated with me on more than a dozen of these recipes. And recipe testers Adelaide Mueller and Sofia Todisco helped tweak, clarify, and improve every one of them.

All the fabulous, fun images were photographed by David Malosh, with Paige Hicks's amazing props, and Simon Andrews's impossibly delicious food styling. The super-helpful illustrations are by Meighan Cavanaugh.

Pro photographer Melanie Dunea shared literal pro tips for *Insta Your Dish*, and also helped recruit awesome kid testers.

Our irrepressible agent, Janis Donnaud, powered the project, as always, with a honed sense of humor and the occasional bolt of lightning.

It takes a lot of cooks to bake words and images into a book. The editorial mix was provided by Doris Cooper, who guided and shaped this cookbook, with Aaron Wehner, Jill Flaxman, and Lydia O'Brien. Stephanie Huntwork, Jan Derevjanik, Terry Deal, Kim Tyner, Marysarah Quinn, and Derek Gullino supplied the red-hot heat of design and production. Marketing and publicity by Stephanie Davis, Windy Dorresteyn, Erica Gelbard, and Kate Tyler got everything onto the plate, and everyone on the unbeatable sales team at Clarkson Potter/Penguin Random House served it to you.

My brilliant editors at *The New York Times* both inspire and support me on a daily basis: Sam Sifton, Emily Weinstein, Patrick Farrell, and Krysten Chambrot.

Most critically, our kids in the kitchen— Bella Baltierra, Lily Beams, Rafa Beams, Dahlia Clark-Gercke, Harry Groves, Jude Martell, and Mason Zelenko—tested the recipes, gave feedback, and made sure the book is kid-ready and kid-friendly. If any of these recipes become a fave, you can thank them when you see them.

A special shout-out to Dahlia for inspiring me and keeping me honest as we cooked together over the years. I can't wait to see what you'll make next.

index